WE LIVED THE DREAM

LEEDS UNITED'S CHAMPIONS LEAGUE ADVENTURE

LAWRENCE O'SULLIVAN

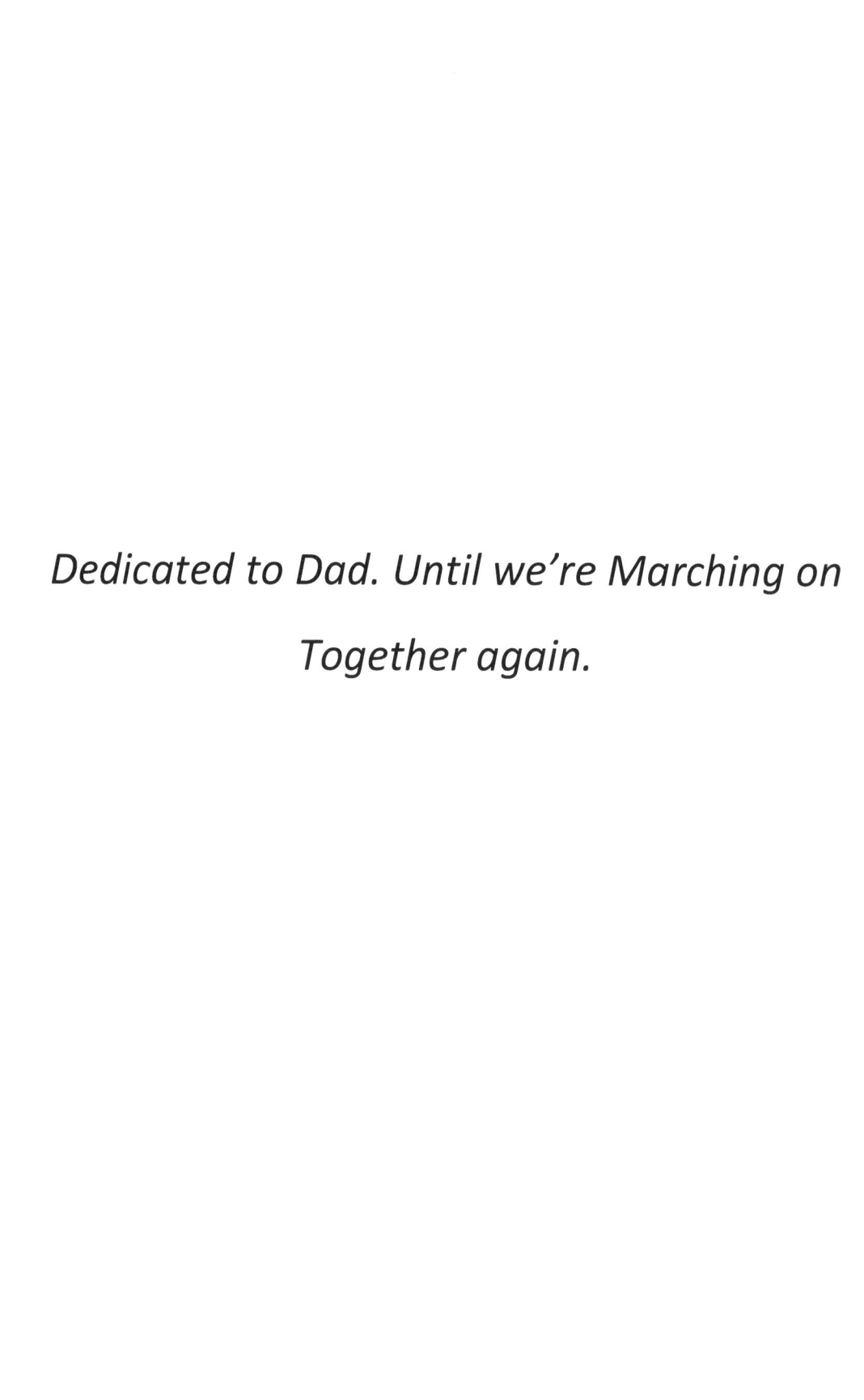

Dedicated to Dad. Until we're Marching on Together again.

Contents

1) Introduction
2) O'Leary's Babies (Part One)
3) O'Leary's Babies (Part Two)
4) The Lions of Munich
5) A Torrid Initiation
6) Singing in the rain
7) A record-equalling win and an unwanted return to Istanbul
8) Last-minute heartbreak
9) Dom Matteo scored a very good goal in the San Siro
10) The Galacticos come to Town.
11) When in Rome
12) Leeds United on Trial
13) Brussels rout
14) Hanging about at the Bernabéu
15) 3-0 to the Weakest Team
16) A Bridge to Far
17) Epilogue - We Lived the Dream.
18) Statistics
19) Sources
20) Authors Note

Introduction

Leeds United's debut season in the 2000-01 Champions League was arguably the most memorable of any team's maiden voyage into Europe's Premier competition since UEFA opted to rebrand and modify the European Cup tournament in 1992. It was a true underdog story of a young enigmatic team made up mostly of academy products with a sprinkling of expensive marquee signings repeatedly defying the odds to nearly go all the way. All the more intriguing was the controversial backdrop it was played against with a high-profile court case - involving star players standing trial over the assault of a student - looming over the football club like a black rain cloud throughout and the tragedy of two of their supporters murdered before a UEFA Cup semi-final against Galatasaray in Istanbul a few months before. Leeds United were front-and-back page news as they became the team everybody was talking about on and off the pitch. Their remarkable campaign saw their supporters have their passports stamped in Europe's most glamourous cities where they saw their heroes strut their stuff in the continent's footballing cathedrals such as the Olympic stadiums of Munich and Rome, Milan's San Siro stadium, Brussels, and a tour of Spain that took in Barcelona and the Camp Nou, Real Madrid, and the Santiago Bernabéu, a nerve-racking evening in La Coruna and culminated at Valencia's Mestalla. There was also the nightmare situation of having to return to Istanbul whilst the wounds of their previous trip were still very much open, an almost unreasonably tricky qualification round, and then being placed not once, but twice in the 'Group of Death' yet emerging unscathed on both occasions. Leeds United can look back at having Barcelona at their mercy in the first group stage and memories of welcoming footballing legends such as

Roberto Carlos, Paulo Maldini, and future Ballon D'or winners Pavel Nedved, Luis Figo and Andrei Shevchenko to their Elland Road home.

The team including players such as Mark Viduka, Alan Smith, Lee Bowyer, Oliver Dacourt, Lucas Radebe, and eventually Rio Ferdinand was iconic for a short period and nearly a quarter of a century on they are still remembered (to coin a social media phrase) as a team that "the streets won't forget". A look at the undeniably Leeds, Nike branded, Strongbow sponsored, classy all-white strip with a subtle yellow and blue trim points immediately to their Champions League odyssey as does their all-yellow collared away kit that was worn on all but one of their trips to the continent. Yet the memory of this team is also one of carelessness and financial irresponsibility from the club's hierarchy that brought the club to its knees a few short years after which almost had fatal consequences for the football club which is still felt somewhat today.

***

Despite the subsequent consequences that the chasing of the sun in this period brought upon Leeds United Football Club, this book aims to be a celebratory account of a near footballing fairytale and a unique chapter in the club's history. It is often criticised that a squad with such talent and one that was eventually so expensively assembled failed to win silverware. However, an argument would be made perhaps — would Leeds supporters would trade the memories of their Champions League campaign for say a League Cup or FA Cup win in that period? Leeds United were the envy of supporters all across the land in the early 2000s.

This book documents the rise of the Elland Road club from Autumn 1998 and the appointment of manager David O'Leary through to their unlikely Champions League semi-final clash with Valencia when at half-time of the second leg Leeds were just one away goal from reaching the final and a date with destiny where they would face a mouthwatering face off with Bayern Munich in which would have been a rematch of the 1975 European Cup Final. That particular match in 1975 was marred with controversy and Leeds United fans still claim the moral victory to this day with a protest chant of "We are the champions, the champions of Europe".

Throughout the book, there will be references to Leeds United's history in European competition dating back to the early 1960s entwined with the 2000-01 season. And to fully understand the magnitude of the run to the semi-finals it is important to consider the nuances of the tournament in the early 2000's and the history of Leeds United leading up to the period.

It can be argued that reaching the Champions League semi-finals in 2000-01 was more of an arduous task than it would be today. Whereas today the top four finishers of the Premier League gain automatic entry to the competition proper, Leeds needed to finish within the top three and their third-place position in 1999/00 only gained them a place in the final qualifying round. Once they reached the competition proper the first round consisted of eight, four-team groups but instead of the top two from each group progressing to a two-legged tie with another team in the last 16 (which was the case for many years until the competition's rejig beginning in the 2024-25 season) there was then a 'second group stage' where there were four more groups of four where the top two progressed to the quarter-finals. That approach brought pros and cons to the table. It meant more matches and thus more income, yet it also brought strain to already congested fixture lists and made repeated qualification arguably more difficult. The format meant a minimum of seventeen European fixtures to reach the final before the second group stage was scrapped in place of eight two-legged ties in the round of 16 in 2003-04. Furthermore, Leeds found themselves drawn into what was widely perceived to be the toughest group in both phases drawing AC Milan, Barcelona, and Beskitas in phase one and their reward for progressing at the expense of Barcelona was European Champions Real Madrid and Italian and Belgian champions respectively - Lazio and Anderlecht.

Playing in Europe was not a novelty for Leeds United then. 2000/01 was their third consecutive year of European football and they were mainstays in Europe for over a decade under the tutelage of legendary manager Don Revie in the late 1960s and early 1970s. Formed in 1919 and with a pretty irrelevant first 40 years of history meandering between the top two divisions before Revie's arrival as first a player and then manager in 1961, Leeds rose from the depths of Division Two to become regular challengers for the league title winning it twice in 1969 and 1974 and finishing runners-up on five more occasions. European travels became the norm, and they added the Inter-Cities Fairs Cup (forerunner to today's Europa League) twice to their trophy cabinet beating Ferencvaros of Hungary in 1968 and Italian giants Juventus in 1971. They reached the final of that competition once more in 1967 and were runners-up in the now-abandoned European Cup Winners Cup losing 1-0 again in controversial circumstances to AC Milan. The European Cup (now UEFA Champions League) was the holy grail to Revie however and the closest he came was a semi-final defeat to Glasgow Celtic in 1970. Revie took the call from his country to lead the England national team in 1974 departing Elland Road after its greatest period of success with Leeds as English Champions. They almost won the European Cup with the squad he built being led by Jimmy Armfield and thought they went 1-0 ahead in the second half in Paris against Bayern Munich only to see Peter Lorimer's goal belatedly ruled offside before the Germans came out 2-0 victors. That game spelled the end of the golden age of Leeds United, and a period of regression ended in relegation from the top flight in 1982. It took Leeds eight years to eventually regain their top-flight status in 1990 under Howard Wilkinson and they immediately marked their territory coming 4th in 1990-91 and then becoming champions again in 1991-92 in the final season before the formation of the Premier League. A poor title defence almost ended in relegation as Leeds failed to win an away game and the chance to consolidate at the top of the league was gone. Patience eventually wore thin with Wilkinson early on in the 1996-97 season and he was dismissed. Replacing him in the hot seat was former Arsenal leader George Graham who brought with him the Gunners' all-time leading appearance maker David O'Leary initially in a playing capacity and then as assistant manager. A season of consolidation was uninspiring although necessary as Leeds finished in eleventh place scoring just 28 league goals all season but at least were stingy at the back (at one point achieving five straight clean sheets including three consecutive goalless draws). An improved season a year later saw them finish in 5th place in 1997-98 and with it UEFA Cup qualification. There was always the premonition that Elland Road was a stopgap for Graham though before a return to London arose which leads into the genesis of one of the most fascinating periods of the club's history to be documented here.

***

There is no question that the club's only involvement in Europe's top competition under the guise of the UEFA Champions League was a remarkable one in a footballing sense despite the controversies that served as a side-show to it. The club may still be paying for the relative success of the run to the semi-finals and Leeds United haven't reached anywhere near those heights in over two decades since and reaching them again any time soon seems unlikely. The author has aimed to write this as an objective account of the period but as a Leeds United supporter, there may be some elements of over-enthusiasm. After all, this is a unique story that Leeds supporters should begin to look back on with pride and not with some distaste and if you're only going to have one stab at the Champions League – you may as well make it this one.

O'Leary's Babies (Part One)

"Georgie, Georgie what's the score?" was the chant ringing around White Hart Lane. It wasn't coming from the Tottenham Hotspur supporters towards their old Arsenal adversary however, but from the Leeds United supporters whose team Graham was in charge of as Leeds went 3-1 ahead against Spurs. All of the media attention before this September Premier League clash revolved around the news that the Scotsman was likely to ditch his post at Elland Road for a return to North London. Graham had been manager at Leeds since the autumn of 1996 and after consolidating an ailing side drifting towards top-flight anonymity in an efficient yet uninspiring first season, in his first full season he led Leeds to fifth place and a return to Europe in the form of the UEFA Cup. Graham signed a lucrative new contract with Leeds in the summer of 1998 worth £1million a year and the same amount for a signing-on bonus. In the early stages of this 1998/99 campaign Leeds were enjoying an unbeaten start and topped the Premier League for the first time since its 1992 rebranding two weeks before the awkwardly timed visit to Spurs with a 3-0 home win over Southampton. There was an underlining feeling however - particularly from chairman Peter Ridsdale - that Elland Road was just a stopgap for him as he returned to management before a more attractive offer arose, after serving a ban following his sacking from Arsenal in 1995 for receiving a 'bung' where he received £400,000 proceeds of the transfers from Pål Lydersen and John Jensen to Arsenal a few years earlier. "I felt George was more committed to success and proving his point than to proving his worth to Leeds United fans. But that hunger for success was something we could harness to our benefit", then Leeds United chairman Peter Ridsdale later quoted in his 2006 autobiography.

Tottenham scored twice in the late stages including a last-minute equaliser from Sol Campbell to draw the game 3-3 to perhaps ease Graham's dilemma. Things came to a head later that week when Ridsdale and Spurs chief Sir Alan Sugar came to an agreement for Graham to join Tottenham with the London club buying out his new contract and signing on bonus and was scheduled to be announced after Leeds's UEFA Cup first-round second-leg trip to Madeira, Portugal to face minnows Maritimo. A distracted Leeds side lost 1-0 but coupled with their identical victory at Leeds in the first-leg the game went to penalties and a 4-1 shoot-out win ensured Leeds progressed to the second round.

Top of the list of replacements for the managerial hot seat was Leicester City's Martin O'Neil and as fate would have it, O'Neil's Foxes were the next visitors to Elland Road. In caretaker charge of United was Graham's assistant David O'Leary. O'Leary - another former Arsenal stalwart - was promoted from a swansong playing capacity at Leeds to a coaching role when his former boss at Highbury took over at Leeds and had enjoyed a good relationship with the players. Far from being media shy, he even had the unusual entity for an assistant manager of a column in the club's official matchday programme. It was expected that O'Leary would follow his old mentor to White Hart Lane but he decided against that to fulfil his duties at Leeds and was pencilled in as one of three candidates for the actual manager's job alongside O'Neil and former Leeds title-winning captain Gordon Strachan who was making an impressive start to management at Coventry City. "The chairman asked me on Wednesday evening if I would be interested in the (caretaker) job. I slept on it and came in on Thursday and he spoke to me about it. He told me the three candidates and I just said "I'll make it easy for yourself, take me out of the ballpark chairman and you're down to two. I think people from that interpreted because you've turned that down you're wanting to go back to London. It's for other reasons I may be able to say at some stage. I'm in a new house, the carpet people are in the wallpaper people are in, so that doesn't tell you that's a person that's trying to get back to London., I've got a contract here for three years to coach the first team and I'll keep doing that and I enjoy doing that until I hear otherwise", O'Leary told the media.

To further strengthen the case for O'Neil to be appointed, his side triumphed 1-0 over Leeds. Leeds was refused permission from Leicester to speak to their manager, but it was known in media and footballing circles that O'Neil was interested in the Leeds job. It was hoped an appointment would be made during a two-week international break. Still, speculation spilled out onto the return of domestic football as O'Leary presided over a 1-1 draw away at Nottingham Forest. Two days later on the 19th of October Leicester came from behind – against, ironically, George Graham's Spurs to win 2-1. The Filbert Street crowd did their utmost to pull on the heartstrings of their dilemma-ridden manager to persuade him to stay with a passionate reception post-match and brandishing banners begging 'Don't leave Martin!'. An emotional O'Neil told the cameras of this televised clash that he had a difficult decision to make in the next 24 hours. By that time, Leeds United were in Rome to face Roma in the first-leg of their second-round clash. It had been confirmed that O'Neil would indeed be staying put at Leicester. O'Leary had to take caretaker charge from the heights of the director's box after receiving a dismissal for his touchline conduct in the previous round at Madeira with Eddie Gray leading from the sidelines. Despite going down 1-0 with ten men after Bruno Riberio's red card, Leeds performed well and twice hit the post in the first-half which practically made the mind up of the Leeds chairman to hand the Irishman the top job. O'Leary was duly appointed despite not winning a game whilst caretaker, before a 0-0 draw with Chelsea on 25th October 1998. "I think I'm hopefully going to be a top-class manager; I want to manage at the top, not lower down, I want to manage at the top where the pressure is. I've played at the top where the pressure is for twenty-odd years and that's where I want to stay for the next twenty years. I know what a privilege it is in your first job to be asked to manage Leeds United. I know the expectations of this club, but I know to take this on we're going to need to invest in some quality players. Not just one of two, but a few", O'Leary said upon his appointment. His first win did eventually come in the next game in a 1-0 defeat of Bradford in the League Cup and a first Premier League victory was secured with a 2-1 win over Sheffield Wednesday.

One of the pleasing aspects of O'Leary's approach for Leeds supporters that was immediately clear was the integration of a crop of exciting youth prospects. Club legend Eddie Gray had led a talented group from the club's revamped academy - set up by Howard Wilkinson - to FA Youth Cup success in 1997 and members of that team were promoted to the first team set up such as Australian winger Harry Kewell, centre back Jonathan Woodgate, midfielders Matthew Jones and Stephen McPhail and goalkeeper Paul Robinson who turned in a man of the match performance against Chelsea on his senior debut in O'Leary's first official match in charge. These starlets were in addition to Lee Bowyer who became Britain's most expensive teenager when he signed from Charlton Athletic in 1996 for £2.8 million. Several of these young charges were trusted in the Elland Road return leg against Roma in which Leeds bravely drew 0-0 but exited the competition on aggregate and then a trip to Anfield where they hadn't won in over twenty years. Among the scorers in a 3-1 victory over Liverpool was an eighteen-year-old striker Alan Smith who scored with his first touch in senior football at the Kop End to level the match at 1-1. He almost repeated the trick a week later when it took him as many as two touches to score in a 4-1 home win over Charlton. The three-game winning streak was halted with an encouraging performance at Old Trafford despite a 3-2 but further wins over West Ham United, Coventry City and Newcastle United and defeats to Arsenal and Blackburn meant Leeds were sat in the top six at the turn of the year.

In this period O'Leary's first signing was one of experience to help compliment the youngsters coming through and was one of immense popularity with supporters. David Batty, the homegrown lynchpin of the 1992 league title-winning team was signed from Newcastle for £4.4 million. Unfortunately, a broken rib (that would eventually cause heart complications) 72 minutes into his debut against Coventry kept him out for three months.

The luck of the FA Cup draw pitched Leeds with Spurs and George Graham in the fifth round and after a 1-1 draw at Elland Road in Graham's first return to Leeds, a 2-0 reverse in North London saw United's old boss win the first duel of master versus apprentice with O'Leary. Graham had signalled that he saw more potential at Tottenham than at Leeds and delivered silverware instantly in the form of the League Cup in March 1999. But in the league, his team were stuttering towards a mid-table finish of eleventh whilst between mid-February and the start of April Leeds would go on a run of seven league victories for the first time since the heydays under Don Revie in the early 1970's. The glorious run earned O'Leary the Manager of the Month award for March and after a goalless draw at home to Liverpool halted the winning habit, Leeds found themselves in fourth place with six games remaining, just six points of leaders Manchester United, four points off Chelsea who were sitting in the third Champions League spot and well ahead of Aston Villa behind in fifth place. A 1-1 draw away at Charlton immediately crushed any optimistic dreams of challenging for the title and even more so when an Andy Cole equaliser cancelled out Jimmy-Floyd Hasselbaink's opener at Elland Road against Manchester United. Leeds won handsomely 5-1 at Upton Park to beat West Ham and keep their Champions League hopes alive but a 1-0 defeat at Chelsea – Leeds's first for ten games - guaranteed the Blues would be heading to the top competition instead and Leeds would have to settle for the UEFA Cup again. On the penultimate game of the season, Leeds faced O'Leary's old club Arsenal at Elland Road. With European qualification secured and Arsenal in a neck-and-neck title race with Leeds's fierce rivals Manchester United, it was wondered if Leeds may take their foot off the gas for the clash and the permutations gave Leeds fans split emotions ahead of the game. Here was another chance to test United's progress against the Premier League's current champions but victory would surely direct the title to Old Trafford. Leeds fan and author Jon Howe told *The Athletic* in 2020, "There was a lot of talk pre-match about Leeds throwing the game and people having moral dilemmas. In reality, it was just posturing. As soon as you got to Elland Road there was no sign of conflicted interests. There was no sense that people wanted Leeds to lose". The Leeds players were also in no charitable mood and were pumped up for this evening's clash under the lights. Ian Harte struck a penalty against the crossbar in first half added time, but Leeds won late on via a late diving header from Jimmy Floyd Hasselbaink at the back post. Despite the bearing on their desired location of the Premier League trophy, it was a true statement of intent from O'Leary's team that they were an up-and-coming force. The season ended with a 2-2 draw with Coventry at Highfield Road and the fourth-place finish represented the club's highest finish since winning the league seven years earlier. It had been a successful breakthrough for the team now christened 'O'Leary's Babies'. But the Leeds manager was yet again adamant that to build on that success would require spending power and not just living off the fruits of the academy. "I'm going to develop this young side and bring them on but it's going to take time and you can't kid yourself that it's going to happen next year or the year after but we haven't any chance of doing it if we're not going to spend money on quality players, what we've got to do is try and consolidate and finish in fourth place again at least and hopefully the lads will get stronger and better and that's the way we're going to do it," O'Leary concluded speaking to the clubs in house season review video.

***

The incomings O'Leary indicated were necessary did come in the summer of 1999 but again youth was the route United travelled down in search of their new additions. Out went Clyde Wijnhard, Bruno Ribiero, Danny Granville, and long-term servant David Wetherall. Through the entrance door came Norway Under 21 captain Erik Bakke joining from his homeland team Sogndal and was cited as one for the future but another injury to David Batty early in the season would open a door for him to play a key role. Long-time target Danny Mills, an England Under 21 defender, joined from relegated Charlton Athletic. O'Leary was told he would have to choose between one of either Ipswich Town winger Kieron Dyer and Chelsea centre-back Michael Duberry with the latter chosen for £4 million. Twenty-one-year-old striker Michael Bridges joined from Sunderland for a handsome £5 million despite being a third-choice striker at his old club behind Kevin Phillips and Niall Quinn as Sunderland won the First Division title the season before. Bridges would however see himself propelled to the role of main striker quickly. Jimmy-Floyd Hasselbaink had been Leeds United's talisman since joining two years prior. Arriving as an unknown entity from Portuguese side Boavista for a fee of £2 million, his 34 goals in 69 appearances were crucial in United's development from mid-table mediocracy to back-to-back European qualifications. His 18 goals in 1998-99 saw him share the Premier League Golden Boot with Michael Owen and Dwight Yorke but demands from Hasselbaink and his agent over a new improved contract brought tension between himself and the club and its supporters. He was jeered during a pre-season friendly at Birmingham City and was subsequently sold for £12 million to Atletico Madrid on the eve of the 1999-00 season opener against Derby County. The fans demanded the £10 million profit be spent on a replacement for the Dutch striker – especially after a goalless draw with Derby - but Leeds held off splashing all of the cash on one superstar marksman but did however purchase Coventry City striker Darren Huckerby for a reputed £6 million.

The calls for a replacement for Hasselbaink quietened and the signing of Bridges looked an astute one when he scored a hat-trick at The Dell in a 3-0 victory over Southampton in the second game of the season. Leeds was handed a tough start to the season and a win over Sunderland at home was sandwiched by a routine 2-0 defeat at Old Trafford to Manchester United and a 2-1 home loss to Liverpool just two days after the Sunderland game. The jaded show for the Liverpool loss was described by O'Leary as the worst performance under his management so far. However, the following run of fixtures saw Leeds go on an unprecedented run of ten consecutive victories in all competitions. Leeds had brushed aside Serbians Partizan Belgrade in the first round of the UEFA Cup 4-1 on aggregate and had one foot in the third round with a thumping 4-1 win over Lokomotiv Moscow at Elland Road in the second-round first-leg. Progression in the League Cup was assured with a 1-0 win over Blackburn Rovers but victories over Tottenham, Coventry, Middlesbrough, Newcastle, Watford and Sheffield Wednesday had lifted Leeds to the summit of the Premier League with 25 points from 11 games by mid-October. The run ended with a thrilling 4-4 draw with Everton at Goodison Park where a last-gasp David Weir equaliser prevented The White's extending their winning run to eleven games. Leeds suffered their first defeat for nearly three months when they were upset by relegation strugglers Wimbledon in a 2-0 defeat at Selhurst Park.

That defeat was just a bump in the road though for Leeds who won their next six Premier League games up to Boxing Day. Within that time frame, Leeds overcame a wasted trip to Moscow to face Spartak which was postponed due to a frozen pitch. It was rescheduled to take place in the Bulgarian capital of Sofia where Leeds fell to a 2-1 defeat in the first-leg before a rare and late Lucas Radebe goal saw Leeds win 1-0 in the return at Elland Road and secure their passage into the last 16 of the UEFA Cup on the away goals rule. After Leeds beat Port Vale 2-0 thanks to a Bakke double in a brought-forward FA Third round tie in December, Leeds was challenging for honours of four fronts. The League Cup became one less option of silverware though when Leeds lost to Leicester City on penalties at 'bogey ground' Filbert Street. Among those six straight Premier League victories, Leeds's young team had shown spirit and determination above their collective years to find ways to win late in games. Winners at home to Southampton and away to Derby were secured in added time. The real statement of Leeds as a force to take seriously though came at Stamford Bridge where their Champions League ambitions died a death six months earlier. A Stephen McPhail double – his first goals in senior football – won Leeds the game 2-0. A 2-1 Boxing Day win over Leicester extended Leeds's lead at the top of the table and despite losing 2-0 to Arsenal at Highbury Leeds United would enter the new millennium sitting proudly at the top of English football.

Leeds would begin the new century with a home defeat to Aston Villa with future England manager Gareth Southgate scoring either side of a Harry Kewell wonder strike. On Sunday 9th January 2000 Leeds travelled to Maine Road to face Manchester City in an interesting FA Cup fourth-round clash that would pit the team at the top of Division One meeting the top of the Premier League. The game lived up to expectations in a pulsating first half which twice saw City take the lead before goals from Alan Smith and Kewell put Leeds ahead 3-2 before the break. A fine second-half performance from Leeds saw them extend their lead to 5-2 with further goals from Lee Bowyer and Kewell had left their fans and media critics purring at the joyfulness of this young enigmatic Leeds United side. In some quarters the current crop of youngsters had been compared to the golden age under Don Revie where players and now club legends such as Paul Reaney, Paul Madeley, Norman Hunter, Peter Lorimier and Eddie Gray to name but a few who had also came through the youth system and stayed at Leeds for over a decade conquering almost all ahead of them. Top of the Premier League, going strong in Europe, through to the FA Cup fifth round – the world was at the feet of O'Leary's team. But by the time they would next take to the field things would never quite be the same for this Leeds team again.

O'Leary's Babies (Part Two)

From one Manchester club to another was meant to be next on the agenda for Leeds as they were originally scheduled to face Manchester United in a top of the table face-off at Elland Road. However, the Red Devils were in Rio de Janeiro for the inaugural FIFA Club World Cup. Their involvement caused great controversy when they decided to give up their defence of the FA Cup in preference of FIFA's new upstart tournament to the great disappointment of football traditionalists in England. This presented a rare fortnight off from action for O'Leary's troops and after the satisfaction of the display and result at Maine Road, O'Leary had granted his players some downtime. Little did he know at the time that the activities of some of his players would change the face of his team and his job forever.

Peter Ridsdale was on business in Hong Kong during the break in the fixture list when he was called by club PR officer Liz Dimitrevic that the Yorkshire Evening Post newspaper was running an exclusive report that Jonathan Woodgate and Lee Bowyer were to be arrested in connection with an assault on a student in Leeds City Centre. He was told at the time that the matter was in hand and that there was nothing to worry about. Three days after the Manchester City game on the evening of 12th January 2000, a 19-year-old student – Sarfraz Najeib - was attacked and left with a fractured left leg, a smashed cheekbone, his nose broken in three places and required twelve stitches for a gash in the back of his head and was left with the indent of teeth marks and the imprint of a shoe on his face. The attack occurred outside the Leeds city centre's Majestik night club where several of the Leeds squad were out. Dimitrevic's assurances to Ridsdale that this was a low-key incident was anything but and Leeds United and its' two young stars in particular were headline news at the start of daily news bulletins and occupying the front pages of the newspapers instead of the back. The news had thrown the football club into chaos and from the unusual entity for Leeds of being everyone's second favourite team thanks to the exciting football and fearless attack on the upper echelons of the Premier League, Leeds United were back in the familiar territory of being reviled and looked at with scorn but for the most serious reason yet. On Monday 17th January, police officers arrived at United's Thorp Arch training ground and said they wanted to interview the two players. Ridsdale had demanded a meeting with his disgraced stars which also included Woodgate's father Alan. Ridsdale recalls in his autobiography - *United We Fall: Boardroom Truths about the Beautiful Game* – that there were tears shed between Woodgate and his father as they realised the seriousness of the situation whereas Bowyer was more nonchalant about it. Bowyer had previous for getting in trouble. Weeks after joining Leeds in 1996 he was convicted of affray and fined £4,500 for throwing chairs around a McDonald's restaurant after a dispute with an Asian employee over his order. The football club was put under pressure to suspend the players immediately. Imran Khan a well-known solicitor for high-profile race-sensitive cases alongside Suresh Grover representing the National Civil Rights movement, Piara Powar from anti-racism organisation *Kick it Out* and Neville Lawrence – father of Stephen – the teenager who was murdered in a racially motivated attack in 1993 – all met with Ridsdale and demanded that the pair were suspended immediately. Despite the pressure, Ridsdale decided against suspending Bowyer and Woodgate with the presumption of 'innocent until proven guilty'. However, whilst their club had stuck with them their country did not. Woodgate already had one England cap to his name and had made several other squads whilst Bowyer's form had him knocking on the door of an international call-up. However, the Football Association had told England manager Kevin Keegan that he was forbidden to pick the pair despite the manager's willingness to do so. Two months later on 14th March 2000, Woodgate and Bowyer were both charged with grievous bodily harm (GBH) and causing affray in Leeds City Centre along with Woodgate's Middlesbrough-based friends Neale Caveney and Paul Clifford. Also involved was Micheal Duberry who had picked up Woodgate and his friends on the night of the attack. Duberry was arrested in March on suspicion of perverting the course of justice as it was claimed that he had lied in a statement to protect his teammate. Reserve team player Tony Hackworth was also arrested in connection with the actual assault.

When football did return for Leeds after their eventful two-week hiatus, they travelled to Sunderland's new Stadium of Light for the first time. Despite being newly promoted 'The Black Cats' were flying high and could move within three points of the league's summit with a win, so it would prove a tricky game for Leeds to get their title challenge back on track after back-to-back defeats in the league. Leeds had added Blackburn Rovers' Premier League title winner Jason Wilcox to their roster before the new year for £4 million and the winger had his first meaningful contribution to the club in his first league start - scoring one and assisting another for Michael Bridges to make a goalscoring return to his old club to give Leeds a much-needed 2-1 victory to stay top of the league.

The distraction of the off-field matters where of no help to Leeds when their on-pitch form then stuttered, firstly exiting the FA Cup away at Aston Villa where a Benito Carbone saw the Midlands club progress 3-2 and then a 3-1 reverse at Anfield helped Liverpool's pursuit of Leeds in the league table. Leeds got back on track against Tottenham with O'Leary again getting the better of his old mentor George Graham in a feisty-tempered 1-0 win at Elland Road, which set up nicely the belated visit of Manchester United next up.

Leeds had missed the opportunity to open up a real gap over their rivals during their stay in Brazil and went into the game on 20th February in second place on 50 points, three behind Manchester United with fourteen games to go. The game was prematurely billed as a title decider, but O'Leary tried to temper expectations and pleaded for some perspective from his team's supporters in his programme notes for the game. "I hope you enjoy today's game and whatever the result, don't get too disappointed or too overjoyed. We are still in the early stages of our development; we have a young side and it's crazy to get carried away at the moment. I've already heard people say that if we finish second or third, we will have missed out. Frankly, that's rubbish", he stated. An Andy Cole goal seven minutes after half-time sealed a 1-0 victory for the visitors but Leeds was left to rue missed chances as Erik Bakke and Harry Kewell were denied by the crossbar and the best chance came and went when Alan Smith struck a post before the ball rebounded out to Bowyer who smashed the ball into the South Stand with an open goal at his mercy. A frustrating goalless draw away at Middlesbrough the next week left Leeds six points adrift of the top spot as their title dreams started to slip fade away, but they still held a significant fourteen-point gap over fourth-place Liverpool for the Champions League places.

Next up was the resumption of European football after the winter break and for the second consecutive year Leeds were pitted up against Italian giants Roma in the UEFA Cup. The previous visit to the Eternal City 17 months before and the subsequent performance in a 1-0 defeat was enough to earn O'Leary his first managerial job. This Last 16 tie was the perfect barometer of how much he and his side had progressed and matured in that period. Nigel Martyn was the hero of the night in the first leg at Rome pulling off numerous stupendous saves to send the tie goalless to Elland Road. Harry Kewell was enjoying a rich vein of form which would see him awarded the PFA Young Player of the Year award at the end of the season and his strike settled the second leg in a famous night for The Whites as they defeated Fabio Capello's more fancied side for a place in the UEFA Cup last eight. Leeds's indifferent form domestically had recovered too. Wins over Coventry City, Bradford City, and Wimbledon kept them in the hunt for second place, and progression to the semi-finals of the UEFA Cup was assured with a 4-2 aggregate win over Czech side Slavia Prague. Filbert Street though was again a place where Leeds came unstuck and a 2-1 defeat to Leicester City and then a 1-0 home defeat to Chelsea all but ended their title challenge with the focus now solely on a top-three finish and Champions League qualification with Arsenal hanging on their coattails in fourth place, three points behind. However, football would soon pale in significance for all involved with Leeds United.

***

Despite the disappointment of a title challenge that looked so promising in January failing to sustain, as April arrived excitement was still high as Leeds prepared for a first European semi-final in 25 years. The other teams making up the final four were French side Lens, Turkish outfit Galatasaray and there was a chance of an all-English tie with Arsenal. It was Istanbul-based Galatasaray who Leeds were drawn against for a place in the Copenhagen final. The away leg was up first and United only had to look to Chelsea's red-hot reception earlier in the same season in the group stage of the Champions League where they were greeted with banners of 'Welcome to Hell' to know that this would be an uncomfortable assignment for O'Leary's young side. It was to become unimaginably uncomfortable on the eve of the match when two Leeds United supporters Kevin Speight and Christopher Loftus were brutally and tragically murdered in Taksim Square in the city's centre. 37-year-old Loftus was announced dead at an Istanbul hospital. Peter Ridsdale was present as the victim's brother identified his body and Speight (40) was in an operating theatre requiring a blood transfusion. Leeds United had paid for more blood to be transferred from another hospital but it was too late as Speight had died as a result of his stab wounds. Leeds had cancelled any flights that weren't already airborne to Istanbul to prevent any more fans from travelling over on matchday. Ridsdale had reasonably requested to UEFA that the match be postponed and rescheduled at a later date. A director from Galatasaray had ludicrously disagreed and the UEFA delegate for the match gave Ridsdale the ultimatum that if Leeds did not fulfil the fixture, then they would forfeit it. Not wanting to allow Galatasaray a free passage into the final and to play for the memory of the late supporters, it was begrudgingly decided Leeds would indeed play the following night. In what was already a harrowing experience for Leeds United's players and supporters they had to endure arguably the most intimidating venue in world football, with the backdrop of tragic circumstances as armoured tanks, water cannons, and riot police with dogs on a leash were all in place with baying mobs of Galatasaray supporters banging on coaches and giving throat-cutting gestures, making the Ali Sami Yen stadium a cauldron of hate. Leeds players came out of the tunnel protected by a wall of riot police defending them from missiles thrown from the stands. The Leeds team were wearing black armbands in honour of Loftus and Speight, but the gesture was not shared by the home team. UEFA had refused requests for a minute's silence as they felt it could provoke the home crowd. Leeds fans inside the stadium instead turned their backs to the action for the first minute of the match. That gesture is still repeated by Leeds fans on the closest game to the anniversary and on the minute of its comparative anniversary and a plaque at Elland Road with the inscription 'They will never be forgotten' sits on the stadium's East Stand. On a night when football was an afterthought Leeds lost 2-0.

On their return to England, Leeds had lost for third time to Aston Villa that season losing 1-0 at Villa Park and Arsenal were the first guests to Elland Road since the tragic events of Istanbul. The newly erected statue of Billy Bremner had become a shrine to the memories of Loftus and Speight with flowers, shirts, and tributes from supporters of all clubs left around its surrounding steps and along the gates and fences of the stadium. In a purely footballing sense, the visit of Arsenal was a key game in the race for a Champions League place. Leeds was sat in the third and final Champions League qualifying place, but Arsenal were only two places and three points behind. But again, a football result wasn't at the forefront of a solemn crowd's mind. The Arsenal team had the grace to present each Leeds player with a bouquet of red and white flowers before the game, but their graciousness stopped there as they romped to a 4-0 victory.

For the return leg with Galatasaray four days later, security was a big talking point pre-match. Directors from Galatasaray had argued that the tie should be removed from Elland Road and played in a neutral venue, but it was decided that Leeds would be allowed to keep their home advantage and the match was played in the absence of any away supporters. An uphill task awaited to reach the final (where Arsenal laid in wait) with a 2-0 deficit. A 2-2 draw in which Erik

Bakke scored a brace was a valiant effort but with Leeds falling 1-0 and 2-1 behind on the night they were never really in contention.

Leeds now had only Champions League qualification on the agenda with five games remaining. They had slipped to their lowest position of fifth place as Arsenal and Liverpool had joined Manchester United in the top three and had Chelsea and Aston Villa breathing down their necks below them for a UEFA Cup place. The run-in started disappointedly as Leeds threw away a 2-0 lead at St. James's Park as Newcastle brought it back to 2-2 before Ian Harte wasted a chance of winning the game when he blasted a penalty wide. But back-to-back wins against soon-to-be-relegated pair Sheffield Wednesday (3-0 away) and Watford (3-1 home) put Leeds back in the driving seat in third place. A win over Everton in the final home game and penultimate league game offered a chance of sealing Champions League qualification after Liverpool were held by Southampton at Anfield the day before. Micheel Bridges had put Leeds ahead with his 21st goal of the season in the first half but Nick Barmby capitalised on a Nigel Martyn error in the second period to equalise. The chance of qualification in front of their own supporters had been squandered but the point did at least mean Leeds would have their fate in their own hands going into the final day as they travelled to East London to face West Ham United. The trip to Upton Park was their 55th and final game of the season and back in West Yorkshire Liverpool headed to Bradford City. Leeds failed to do their bit as they drew 0-0 at Upton Park and were therefore left at the mercy of their West Yorkshire neighbours to spring an upset against Liverpool. Bradford needed a win to preserve their Premier League status and they achieved that through the unlikely source of former Leeds United captain David Wetherall scoring the winner. On the coach back up north after the game, the Leeds team had rung their former teammate signing "Wetherall, Wetherall" with the

Bradford defender happy he was able to contribute to the success of both his new and old employers.

It had been a remarkable season for David O'Leary and his team who had dared to dream but perhaps a lack of experience and the off-field events of the Majestik nightclub incident and the horrors of Istanbul all contributed to an exhausting second half of the campaign finishing 22 points off league winners Manchester United in the end. But third place was an improvement of 1998/99's fourth and again the club's best effort since the formation of the Premier League and Leeds could now look ahead to mixing it with Europe's elite the next season. "This was a reward for a young team, and I didn't think we'd make it this season. Three-quarters of the way across the ocean the engines failed, and we only just limped into port", O'Leary said using a marine analogy to summarise his team's achievement.

The Lions of Munich

1860 Munich

UEFA Champions League 3rd Qualifying Round

When the final whistle blew at Upton Park at the end of the previous season and with third place secured, everyone involved with Leeds United could be forgiven for their celebrations believing Champions League football had been secured even though realisation would have eventually hit that third place in the Premier League back then only meant entry into the competition's qualifying stages. The White's exploits in reaching the UEFA Cup semi-finals in 1999/00 meant they were spared the opening two rounds of qualifying and would enter the third and final round of qualification. English teams that played out these play-offs previously had found the seeding system to pair them with favourable opposition from the minnow leagues of European football and with it a relatively gentle passage to the competition proper in games which would take place at the very beginning of the domestic season in England. In the previous year at this stage, Chelsea were paired with Latvian side Skonto FC whom they brushed aside 3-0 on aggregate and the year before that Manchester United, who had the rare scenario of not gaining automatic entry eased past Polish outfit LKS Lodz.

Therefore, when Peter Ridsdale and David O'Leary travelled to Nyon, Switzerland on 21st July and with Leeds being listed as a seeded team they would have envisaged a similar type of opposition standing between them and a debut in the Champions League. Among the other seeded sides, Leeds needed not to worry about included Italian giants Inter and AC Milan, Scottish neighbours Glasgow Rangers, losing finalists from the previous season

Valencia, experienced Dutch European travellers Feyenoord and thankfully there was no chance of an immediate return to Turkey and Galatasaray.

Looking at the unseeded half of the draw, despite some still strong opposition as you would expect from the cream of the European Leagues, there were plenty of ties available in which Leeds would have fancied their chances. Austrians Trol Innsbruck, Polish side Polonia Warsaw, Hungarian champions Dunaferr, and Romanians Zimbru Chisinau would have hardly struck fear into the contingent representing Leeds at the draw. However, when the balls were pulled out of the Perspex bowl Leeds had learned they would have an arduous early first hurdle to get past Germans 1860 Munich who had finished fourth in the previous season's Bundesliga standings just below TSV Hamburg (who could of also of drawn Leeds but instead beat Brondby from Denmark 2-0 on aggregate).

United would have to negotiate a tricky assignment before the celebrations and plans for extended travels across the continent could begin. Ridsdale was wary of the scale of the task and stated, "I think it's one of the toughest ties we could have had at this stage". O'Leary had travelled to Germany to see 1860 in action and was also aware of a team who were "big, strong and tough" and assessed that "when you think that we finished in third place in England, and they were the fourth team in Germany this could easily have been a UEFA Cup quarter-final tie". 1860 had some notable talent in their ranks including the previous season's Bundesliga golden boot winner Martin Max and German international midfielder Thomas Hassler, a free-kick specialist, who possesses winners' medals from the World Cup in 1990 and Euro 96.

In that respect, you would have envisaged that 1860 Munich, although arguably escaping an even harder draw than Leeds United, would have been equally underwhelmed with their reward for reaching the qualification places in one of the world's classiest leagues. Instead, their Norwegian midfielder Erik Myland was quoted as saying "I don't think that Leeds are that good", - the first in a long series of underestimations of O'Leary's men throughout the campaign.

* * *

Leeds had already started their preparations for building on their best Premier League-era finish and started building a squad that they hoped could compete with an extensive domestic and European schedule. The club had smashed its' record outlay for a transfer, paying French team RC Lens £7.2 million for the services of former Everton midfielder Olivier Dacourt who posed with a shirt displaying the digits of the fee alongside a gleeful Peter Ridsdale. Australian striker Mark Viduka was recruited from Glasgow Celtic to spearhead the attack costing a sizeable for the time £6 million and they then persuaded Liverpool defender Dominic Matteo away from Anfield for £4.25 million, a signing O'Leary would later reflect to be the bargain buy of the season. Another Australian, Jacob Burns was brought for a quarter of a million pounds from now-dissolved Aussie club Parramatta Power to boost the squad.

Leeds had recouped some of the outlay with outgoing transfers. Martin Hiden returned to his homeland of Austria with SV Salzburg and former key players who were now moved to the fringes were moved on bringing in £6.3 million. Alfie Haaland moved across the Pennines to Manchester City and David Hopkin and Robert Molenaar both across West Yorkshire to Bradford City. The net spending of £11.4m represented sensible business in the transfer market at the time for Leeds, perhaps the last time that could be said under this particular regime.

Leeds had begun their preparations for the season dipping their toes in the water with a three-game tour of Sweden against average local opposition. A 5-3 goal-fest was played out with Panos Ljungskile SK before Lysekils FF and Jonkoping Sandra IF were well beaten 7-1 and 5-1 respectively. Back in blighty, Leeds beat Nottingham Forest 2-1 at the City Ground before an Ian Harte hat-trick was the difference in a 3-2 win at former Premier League champions, but now second-tier Blackburn Rovers. In total Harte had scored an impressive total of eight goals in these friendlies from his position of left-back including converting penalties and his trade-mark free-kicks. Leeds wrapped up the pre-season programme with a short dash past Wooley Edge Services for a 2-0 win at Huddersfield Town. Attention now turned to competitive matters and the small matter of reaping the rewards of the previous season and qualifying for the biggest and best club competition of them all.

* * *

The 'Lions of Munich', predictably formed in 1860 with vast support from a working-class background had and have since shared similarities to Leeds where they could easily adopt for themselves the line from United's famous Marching on Together chant where they twice exclaim for effect "and we've had our ups and downs". When the German Bundesliga was reformed in 1963, 1860 Munich was the team to shout about in Bavaria. More so than their neighbours Bayern Munich who had yet to find the success they are now synonymous with now. They were German Champions in 1965-66 but older English fans would have remembered 1860 from their meeting with West Ham United at Wembley in the now defunct European Cup Winners Cup. That game served almost like a dress rehearsal for the World Cup Final in the same stadium twelve months later, with a game involving an English side fielding

Bobby Moore, Geoff Hurst and Martin Peters playing German opposition and the game ending with Moore being carried on his teammate's shoulders - holding the cup aloft just as he later would with the Jules Rimet trophy. As the 1960's turned to the 70's Bayern had overtaken their neighbours winning three back-to-back league titles from 72-74 and three consecutive European cups from 74-76. Meanwhile, 1860 plunged into a string of financial crisis and in 1982 they eventually lost their professional status dropping into the amateur Bavarian regional league. (Incidentally, they again suffered the same fate in 2017 dropping into the Regionalliga but they made an instant return and currently ply their trade in the third tier, the 3. Liga.) In 1992 they were brought by millionaire Karl-Heinz Wildmoser and hired Werner Lorant as manager and the pair guided the Lions back to the top-flight in 1994. High on the clubs' resurgence, Lorant then said the next goal was the Champions League causing even their own supporters to laugh at their coach's optimism. However, they were now just a two-game shoot-out away from achieving that most unlikely of comebacks.

***

A mere 87 days after the 1999/00 Premier League season had ended Elland Road was geared up to stage European football for the third consecutive season but this time for their first foray into Europe's premier competition for eight years and their first since the European Cup was rebranded as the Champions League. There wasn't the famous classical anthem for the players to line up to in one of the more popular pre-match rituals in football, nor was there the competition's logo (a ball made up of connecting stars) dressing up the stadium alongside a plastering of UEFA's select group of sponsors. All of this was reserved for the first group phase which would be the reward for the winners of the tie, while the losers would enter the first round of the UEFA Cup. A crowd of 33,769 - including a couple of thousand travelling from Germany situated in the South Stand - was seven thousand below capacity - and if it wasn't for the high stakes, you could be forgiven for thinking it was an extension of the pre-season programme with the Premier League season still due to kick off in ten days time.

David O'Leary was unable to call upon numerous key players for this crunch game to open the season. Eleven days before the game only ten first-team players completed a training session owing to an injury crisis. "We've picked up a lot of injuries at the wrong time of the year and as the qualifying game is so near, I admit that I am now worried," O'Leary said speaking to Don Warters. Speaking before the game the Leeds gaffer said what it would take to navigate through the tie given the number of absences. "In some ways, we have to try to limit the damage in the first leg and keep a clean sheet and then hope for a miracle that will bring some of our missing players back for the second leg". Leeds would be missing the services of wingers Harry Kewell and Jason Wilcox, long-term resident to the physio room David Batty, and midfielders Matthew Jones and Stephen McPhail. Leeds had recruited a highly rated physiotherapist Dave Hancock over the off-season and even he was astonished by the injury situation. "It was a nightmare situation. I'd not experienced anything quite like it in my time in the game," he said.

Speaking in the matchday programme O'Leary used his notes section to state that his target for his team for the season was to make the top three of the Premier League again and if Leeds could first qualify and then make it out of the first group phase it would represent a "marvellous achievement and anything after that would be a bonus".

Unfortunately, the match would be overshadowed by a terrible performance from the Cypriot referee Costas Kapitanis in a game that saw him lose control of the game and administer three red cards. Leeds took control of the game in the closing stages of the first half after taking the lead on 40 minutes through Alan Smith. A long kick-up field from Nigel Martyn was won by Mark Viduka, who was making his competitive debut for the club despite not being fully match-fit to help aid the injury crisis. His knocked-on header confused the Munich defence and as centre-back Martin Stranzi tried to head home to his goalkeeper Michael Hoffmann - who had come to collect the ball - he was pipped to it by Smith who reacted quickest and headed home. It was Smith's first goal since January of that year and as he wheeled away, arms stretched out in celebration, commentator for Sky Sports Alan Parry reminded those watching at home that every time Smith had scored, Leeds had gone on to win. Leeds gained further control a few minutes later when they found themselves with a goal and a man advantage. Kewell and Viduka's Australia national teammate Ned Zelic had made two late challenges and the second on Ian Harte alongside the touchline was perhaps more worthy of just a warning but was instead shown a second yellow card. It was an unwelcome return to West Yorkshire for the Aussie who had played a couple of trial matches at Leeds a couple of years previously.

Things continued to go swimmingly for United after half-time and they looked to take even further control of the tie on 71 minutes. The Leeds fans were treated to a first glimpse of some neat link-up play between Smith and Viduka and the latter charged towards the penalty box before being clipped down. Kapitanis pointed to the penalty spot incensing the Munich players and replays showed the offence happened just outside the box. Ian Harte stepped up for the fortunate spot kick and continued his incredible summer goal-scoring form, waiting for Hoffmann to make the first move before passing into the opposite corner of the net.

From this position of strength, everything started to go wrong for Leeds. Olivier Dacourt, also making his competitive debut in all white, was booked for a challenge on Marco Kurz shortly after the break but it seemed he had got a touch of the ball before his marker. This time, on 75 minutes, as Leeds chased a third goal the Frenchman charged towards Kurz again and fell to the ground as his opponent stuck out a leg to tackle. The referee had considered it an act of simulation and issued a second yellow card to restore parity in terms of the number of players on each side. That parity vanished shortly after, and it was suddenly Munich who found themselves with an advantage in personnel. Erik Bakke, who was cautioned earlier in the game jumped up for a header in the opposition's penalty area with his arm raised which unintentionally struck the ball and Kapitanis blew and gave the disbelieving Norwegian his marching orders too. Andy Gray co-commentating for Sky Sports couldn't believe the display of refereeing he was witnessing. "Ridiculous, staggering, it's worse than that it's worrying", was his description of the Cypriot's performance.

With seven minutes, plus added time, remaining Elland Road and Leeds United went into insurance mode happy to protect their two-goal lead and see the game out. Whilst two goals ahead, everyone inside the stadium knew what ramifications a late 1860 away goal would have on the tie overall. Whistles were heard around the ground hoping that the hapless Kapitanis would also blow his whistle as the game approached a fourth minute of added time. A lofted cross in from the left side flew into the penalty area where Lucas Radebe wasn't tight enough to his marker- the Australian Paul Agostino - who had a previous spell in England with Bristol City - whose downward header beat

Martyn and stunned and silenced Elland Road. It was the last act of the game, and the final whistle was greeted by cheers and high fives amongst the visiting contingent. Leeds knew that they would have it all to do in a fortnight in Bavaria as just a 1-0 defeat would see them dumped out of the Champions League at the first hurdle. They would now also have the added complications of Dacourt and Bakke's suspensions to contend with alongside the ever-growing injury list.

O'Leary was only too aware of what a setback that late Agostino goal and the suspensions were to Leeds. "The late away goal they scored was a big blow and we need to get that back as soon as we can over there. We've got a great spirit in the club, and you can be sure we will be giving everything to go through". He was also already looking ahead to who he could even pick for the return in Munich. "I don't mean this as a joke, but I don't know what side I can field for that game. I'm not very confident about going through it. I'm not being defeatist I'm just being realistic. It's no way to be going into the biggest game this club has had without nine players", was his frank assessment. It was a sound assessment but perhaps also a nudge for his chairman to support the man Ridsdale called "the best young manager in the business", with O'Leary often bemoaning at this stage the club's lack of spending power compared to the likes of Chelsea and Manchester United.

His 1860 Munich counterpart Werner Lorant was much more buoyant. Despite the 2-1 defeat, his team were now favourites to qualify. "If someone had said before the game that we could have a 2-1 score line from the first leg then I would have been happy to have taken it", he said.

The referee's performance was unsurprisingly the main talking point after the match. Erik Bakke had his say on his dismissal from the game and the two others that occurred. "My sending off, I thought it was a joke. The referee was as bad for Munich as he was for us. I don't think any of the dismissals were deserved". Dacourt was too disappointed with his sending-off but suggested he was "more disappointed about conceding a late goal than the sending-off".

Kapitina's performance did not go unnoticed by the official UEFA match delegate in attendance, Ferreira De Sequeira. He had a meeting with Kapitinas in the match officials' dressing room at Elland Road which lasted half an hour and was quoted to the media as saying, "We are fully aware that the game was handled poorly by the referee. There will be a complete investigation into why his performance was so bad".

Nevertheless, Leeds had lost control of a tie that they had a firm grip on and would now have it all to do in Munich.

***

Munich's Olympiastadion was an impressive yet unusual setting for a football stadium with its striking acrylic glass roof canopy covering two-thirds of it, making it look somewhat like the canopies found at Butlins resorts. It had been home to 1860 since 1995 when they moved from their beloved Stadion an der Grünwalderstraße (also referred to as *Sechzgerstadion*, meaning "60er Stadium") to the Olympiastadion where they would ground share with city rivals Bayern Munich. Some fans were still aggrieved to leave their former home so much that they would meet at the *Sechzgerstadion* and travel to the Olympiastadion on matchdays. Subsequently, they have since moved back to their spiritual home in 2017.

The stadium also had the always unwelcome sight of an athletic track around the pitch, distancing supporters from the action. This was due to it being purpose-built for the 1972 Summer Olympics. Two years later, it hosted the 1974 World Cup final where West Germany overcame Johan Cruyff's Netherlands team. Fourteen years after that, the Netherlands made a glorious return to the stadium winning EURO 1988 courtesy of Marco Van Basten's audacious volley from the most acute of angles. It had also hosted three European Cup finals and 13 months after Leeds United's visit, a Michael Owen hat-trick helped England to a memorable 5-1 thrashing of Germany in a crucial World Cup qualifier. Both 1860 and Bayern moved away from the historic stadium in 2005 to the Allianz Arena - purpose-built for football ahead of Germany hosting the 2006 World Cup.

After the first leg, O'Leary had described the second-leg clash as "the biggest game this club has had". It was a bold statement for a club that has won three league championships and competed in no less than five European finals across various competitions. But from a financial perspective, he was arguably correct. Not only would the winners of the tie qualify for the Champions League they would also pocket a cool £10m.

Since the first leg, Leeds had kicked off their Premier League campaign with a 2-0 home win over Everton courtesy of two Alan Smith goals. The Rothwell-born youngster burst on the scene two seasons previously when he came off the bench to score with his very first touch in professional football at Anfield in a 3-1 win over Liverpool and had an impressive rookie season. However, his manager described his first full season in 1999/00 as a "bad one" and there were noises that he could leave Leeds in the summer of 2000 with Manchester City manager Joe Royle, newly promoted to the top-flight, sending admiring glances. But O'Leary and Ridsdale insisted he had a future at Leeds and after a successful operation on a troublesome ankle, he staked a claim to play a big part in Leeds's season this time round.

The Leeds contingent arrived the day before the game and as with every European tie had the chance to train on the stadium's pitch. These final preparations would have been insubstantial compared to those of 1860 Munich who were rumoured to have been training four times on the eve of the match and twice on actual match day in preparation for the crunch tie.

A 56,000 thousand crowd packed the stands of the Olympiastadion including an impressive 2,5000 Leeds fans. For fans watching back home the match was aired on an obscure pay-per-view channel and amongst those viewers were the injured Dominic Matteo and the suspended Erik Bakke in the former's living room calming their nerves with bottles of beer. Matteo admits in his autobiography – *In My Defence* – that the pair were "kicking every ball". As funny as it sounds now, the lure of Champions League football was what persuaded Matteo to trade his beloved Liverpool for Leeds United as he had never experienced the competition with the Anfield club.

O'Leary admitted that getting through this tie would be the most difficult task of his career to date but would have to patch up a line up with only Lee Bowyer as a recognised natural midfield player. Gary Kelly, a right-back by trade was pushed to the right side of midfield, and central defender Lucas Radebe adopted a central midfield role. Youngster Matthew Jones, who would be moving to pastures new at Leicester City shortly after, partnered Radebe in midfield and Lee Bowyer took up the left side.

Once the game kicked off, the game played out how some at Leeds had expected with a confident Munich side enjoying possession and laying siege on the Leeds goal. Goalkeeper Nigel Martyn admitted between the two legs that in the first leg Leeds tried to refrain from conceding free-kicks close to their goal due to the quality that Munich's Thomas Hassler possessed from dead-ball situations. "Our chief scout Ian Broomfield had watched the Munich team and he mentioned to me before kick-off that I should watch out for Hassler trying to bend free-kicks round the wall", Martyn said. Broomfield's advice came to fruition when shortly before half-time Hassler was successful in bending one of his trademark free-kicks around the Leeds defensive guard onto a post, but Martyn was there to gather the ball safely in his hands and kiss the ball full of relief, humouring both Bakke and Matteo back home.

Assistant manager Eddie Gray explained in his autobiography, *'Marching on Together – My life with Leeds United'*, how he and O'Leary had tweaked their line up to neutralise 1860 winger Harald Cerny who had given Ian Harte problems in a nervous first half. Harte, a left back was swapped with the right back Danny Mills who "was more of a natural defender" moving to the left, Gray explained.

Gray was a joyful winger from the legendary Don Revie era when passports were a necessary item for being in the Leeds United team who competed in Europe for ten successive seasons. On this occasion, three of his former teammates John Giles, Joe Jordan and Peter Lorimer were part of the media entourage to cover the game from a Leeds perspective. It took 30 seconds after the restart for them to report on a crucial Alan Smith goal that put United in full control of the tie. From the kick-off, the ball found Cerny out wide who ran down the right side of the pitch and lofted a cross into the Leeds penalty area which was gathered by Martyn who sent a long kick up field into the Munich defence. In a similar fashion to the first goal at Elland Road a fortnight earlier, Viduka hassled centre-back Stephan Passlack who scuffed his clearance and nudged the ball through the legs of his defensive partner Marco Kurz. Smith collected the ball and steadied himself before converting past Hofmann to send the Leeds fans behind the goal, but still a distance away due to the athletic track on the pitch's perimeter, into ecstasy. Smith hurdled an advertisement board and entered the track to share the moment with the travelling fans.

The goal meant that Munich now needed to score two goals to force extra-time or three to win the game outright but had pretty much an entire half to chase the game. Chase the game they did, and it took a heroic rear-guard action from the men dressed in all yellow, to keep Munich from producing a comeback. Jonathan Woodgate, Michael Duberry and Mills all cleared a shot apiece off the line and Martyn made a man-of-the-match performance in keeping a clean sheet making numerous saves - the pick of the bunch a one-handed effort to deny Daniel Borimirov.

Leeds's patched-up troops had weathered the storm however and the final whistle was a signal that Leeds had made it to the Champions League group phases against the odds. "Overcoming the fourth best team in Germany, over two legs – especially with playing resources stretched to breaking point", O'Leary summariesed, justifying what he would later describe as the finest achievement across the European campaign.

As the Leeds fans and players celebrated their victory, a sour altercation between the two managers led O'Leary to call his opposite number Werner Lorant a man "who would have few challengers as the most arrogant coach in Europe". The German coach, who had worked wonders promoting 1860 Munich from the depths of the German regional leagues to this two-game play-off for a place on the biggest stage in football, completely blanked his colleague in the away dug-out and refused to shake hands.

Eddie Gray was full of praise for the young contingent in the Leeds line up that he had helped nurture through the academy. "The young players who came in, some of whom hadn't had any experience at this level, were superb and played their parts to the full in helping to achieve what has to be a fantastic result", he applauded.

Notable teams also joining Leeds United into the first group phase from the other qualifying rounds would be AC Milan, fellow Brits Glasgow Rangers, last season's finalists Valencia, UEFA Cup holders Galatasaray and 1860's German counterparts TSV Hamburg. Inter Milan had fallen at this hurdle to Swedes Helsingborg 1-0 on aggregate and Portuguese side Porto who would later win the competition four years later failed to get past Anderlecht of Belgium.

Leeds United had won their golden ticket to the fanciest party in Europe and would soon find out that they would be sharing a table with some very prestigious guests.

A Torrid initiation

UEFA Champions League, 1st Group Phase. Matchday One

Vs Barcelona (Away)

Two days after the victory in Munich, the draw for the Champions League's first group stage took place in the billionaire's playground of Monaco. A draw in any competition for an underdog brings the same dilemma, be it minnows making it to the third round of the FA Cup or this case a Leeds United side dipping its toes in shark-infested waters for the first time. Naturally, there is the allure of the opportunity to play against a giant, a team you would never otherwise get the opportunity to play against, or a mega stadium for a place for fans to visit. But what if you could get a favourable draw and maybe meet those teams deeper into the competition? Those thoughts would of no doubt of been in the mind of the Leeds entourage including Peter Ridsdale and club secretary Ian Silvester in Monaco that afternoon. Leeds was among a group of teams making their debut in the Champions League group stage rebranded in 1992 alongside Spanish champions Deportivo La Coruna, 1983 European Cup winners TSV Hamburg, Heerenveen, Helsingborg, Lyon and Shakhtar Donetsk.

Being placed predictably in Pot 3 of the draw, Leeds could expect a tricky group for their debut campaign but they would never have expected quite what was to come. As the balls were being pulled out of the bowl and the draw was taking shape, Group H had already paired Barcelona and AC Milan in the same group. Silvester admits he and Ridsdale were joking saying "We don't want that one. Then our name came out of the hat, and there was a huge gasp across the room. After the way we played in the UEFA Cup last season, Leeds United were well respected now and a lot of teams did not want to play us", he said. If being paired with two of the biggest clubs in world football wasn't enough to make the mouth water, there was added drama when Turkish side Besiktas completed Group H meaning Leeds and their travelling supporters would be subjected to a return to Istanbul just months after the horrific night when two supporters were murdered there on the eve of their UEFA Cup semi-final with Galatasaray.

Chairman Ridsdale was delighted with the group and as a Leeds United supporter himself he was excited for the fans who have "dreamed of being able to see teams such as Barcelona and AC Milan play at Elland Road and to have both of them in the same group is very special". The pairing with Besiktas brought with it the obvious complications and other than being paired with Galatasaray themselves, it was an unfortunate event that would need to be managed.

Despite the 'Group of Death' indeed looking like a death sentence to United's hopes of further progression in the competition, the players were delighted with the prospect of mixing it with European royalty. Jason Wilcox reflected on the draw before the Barcelona game stating that he thought the draw was a "tremendous" one and that "all the lads wanted to be drawn against the big teams because we felt we were capable of doing well against them. A whole generation has grown up since the team Don Revie built competed in the European Cup so it would be nice for them if we could write our own piece of Champions League history", said the Leeds winger.

Dominic Matteo recalled the team's reaction to the draw in his autobiography *In My Defence*. "We had been hoping to draw at least one of the big boys, as every professional footballer worth his salt wants to test himself against the best. But we didn't just get one, we got two – Barcelona and AC Milan. I was getting treatment for my injured knee when our name was drawn out in Group H so was one of the first to know. I am told the lads, on being told out on the training field, at first didn't believe the news. This was the stuff dreams were made of".

***

Once the fixtures were released, Leeds discovered their first assignment was the away game at Barcelona. Leeds United could claim to have an interesting history with the Catalan giants and as a club, they were no strangers to the impressive surroundings of the enormous Camp Nou stadium having played there three times previously. In 1971 having just won the Inter-Cities Fairs Cup with victory over Juventus, they possessed a trophy of a now-defunct competition, after the equivalent tournament became the UEFA Cup (now known as the Europa League). With the trophy being won by no team permanently, a one-off play-off tie was arranged between the current holders (Leeds) and the winners of the first Inter-Cities Tournament which happened to be a 'Barcelona XI' back in 1958 when they defeated a 'London XI' including the legendary Jimmy Greaves and Johnny Haynes 8-2 on aggregate. The game was arranged to be staged in Barcelona in front of a half-full Nou Camp of 45,000 with Barcelona defeating Don Revie's men 2-1 with two Teőfilo Duenas goals either side of a Joe Jordan strike. The 'Trophee Noel Beard' is now held on display in the Camp Nou's expansive museum.

Four years later Leeds experienced one of the most glorious nights in their history when they against all odds reached the European Cup final with a 1-1 draw in a semi-final 2nd leg complimenting a 2-1 success at Elland Road in the first leg. Peter Lorimer stunned a 100,000 Catalan crowd scoring after seven minutes and putting Leeds two goals ahead in the tie. It was backs-against-the-wall stuff from that point on however especially when Gordon McQueen was shown a red card for violent conduct and were against the ropes when Manolo Clares netted shortly after. 10-man Leeds held on however and reached the final showpiece in Paris for the first time.

Their most recent and most curious visit to the Catalan capital was eight years previous in 1992. Fresh from winning an improbable league title Leeds were in Europe's top competition for the first time since reaching that final in 1975. They looked to have fallen at the first hurdle however against German Champions Stuttgart. A 3-0 defeat in Germany was valiantly fought back with a 4-1 win at Elland Road but Stuttgart's goal in the second leg meant that Leeds went out on the away goals rule. That was until the day after the game when it was brought to attention that Stuttgart had broken the rule that was in place where only three foreign players could be fielded in European matches. In an attempt to arrest the torrential barrage of pressure Leeds was applying, Stuttgart's General Manager Christoph Daum sent on Yugoslav defender Jovo Simanic for his only appearance for the club, and in doing so fielded their fourth non-German player. The British press, never ones to miss a trick, predictably dubbed the Stuttgart boss 'Christoph Dumb'. UEFA awarded Leeds an obligatory 3-0 win instead of directly disqualifying the Germans which produced the dilemma of how to settle the tie as it was stuck at 3-3 on aggregate. A play-off was hastily arranged in the neutral surroundings of Barcelona's Nou Camp. It was an unnecessarily large venue for fans of teams who would have to make hasty travel arrangements and sacrifices to which only 20,000 attended (a fifth of the capacity) but it was a welcome opportunity for the Leeds players to grace one of the great stadiums in world football. Carl Shutt was the unlikely hero for Leeds coming off the bench to score the winner in a 2-1 victory to set up a second-round battle of Britain clash with Glasgow Rangers.

***

Barcelona have always been considered one of the giants of European Football but back in 2000 success in the European Cup was often frustratingly out of reach. Only once at this stage had they laid their hands on the famous trophy back in 1992 when Johan Cruyff's 'Dream Team' defeated Sampdoria before their Lionel Messi-inspired, further four triumphs between 2006 and 2015. They were however a team to fear with a star-studded line-up. World Player of the Year Rivaldo was in their ranks alongside his impressive strike partner Patrick Kluivert. The close season brought fractions between the club president Joan Gaspart and their supporters right from the opening day of his presidency when fan favourite Luis Figo was transferred to arch-enemies Real Madrid. The transfer so upset the Barcelona fans that when Figo returned to the Camp Nou two years later he found a pig's head thrown in his direction when he was taking a corner. The fee recovered for Figo was however spent impressively as they used it for a double swoop at Highbury, taking Arsenal's Marc Overmars and World Cup winner Emmanuel Petit for a combined £54 million. They also had a young Carles Puyol and Xavi Hernandez in their ranks and were captained by a certain Pep Guardiola although none of the trio would feature in this game.

Barcelona had only just kicked off their La Liga campaign the weekend before and opened their season with a 2-1 home win over Malaga courtesy of two Rivaldo goals. Leeds meanwhile had initially built on their opening-day victory over Everton and their qualification in Munich with an away win at

Middlesbrough. However, they had slipped up in their past two games, first losing at home 2-1 to newly promoted Manchester City and then playing out a 0-0 draw with Coventry City at Highfield Road. Barcelona had enjoyed recent good fortune against English sides in Europe. In the previous 1999/00 season's campaign, they had beaten both Arsenal and Chelsea en route to the semi-finals where they lost out to fellow Spaniards Valencia. At this point, Liverpool was the only English side to of beaten Barcelona at their illustrious home.

Like in Munich, Leeds was travelling to Barcelona with a depleted squad. Harry Kewell, Jonathan Woodgate, Erik Bakke, and Dominic Matteo still occupied the Thorp Arch treatment room whilst the only players in the squad with Champions League experience, Wilcox and David Batty (both with Blackburn Rovers) were also unavailable. Mark Viduka, brought to spearhead United's attack at this level was missing for the opening exchanges of the season as he was representing Australia at their home Sydney Olympic Games much to O'Leary's frustration.

O'Leary admitted his frustrations and his worry for Leeds's chances when travelling to his "favourite club and favourite city" and that his team could be on the end of a six-goal beating in his book *Leeds United on Trial*. "On the way over to Spain, I heard people predicting that we might get a draw at the Nou Camp. Either they were anticipating a football miracle, or they were kidding themselves, we didn't stand a chance with so many players missing. It was like going to war with a popgun", he said.

The Leeds manager was frustrated with the arrogance of his opposite number Werner Lorant against 1860 Munich and this time had gripes with Barcelona over what he perceived as arrogance over the calibre of their club and their "we'll do things our way" attitude. For example, there were new rules brought

In by UEFA to ensure the dimensions of the pitch would have to be the same in every ground. The pitch at the Nou Camp is famed for its giant size and the vast surroundings were very different from the close and intimate proximity of Elland Road. When taking their obligatory training session on the pitch on the eve of the match, Leeds's management team had informed the UEFA delegate in charge that no changes had yet been made but were assured that it would be done by kick-off. "It was supposed to be shortened by a few yards, with four yards taken off the width, but needless to say, hardly anything had happened. About half a yard was taken off the width. It was a token gesture", O'Leary wrote in *Leeds United on Trial*.

The travelling Leeds supporters, still able to dress in shorts under the late summer Spanish sun, took their seats high up in the gods of the Camp Nou stadium where the players would look more like *Subbuteo* players without the use of binoculars as a crowd of 85,000 (well over double the capacity of Elland Road) awaited kick-off. It was somewhat of an understrength line up for the Whites which read Martyn, Mills, Radebe, Duberry, Harte, Bowyer, McPhail, Dacourt, Kelly, Smith, and Bridges. But most telling was the lack of depth with the substitutes bench consisting of fringe players and youngsters from the academy. Leeds started the opening exchanges aggressively opting to try and attack their opponents rather than sit back and soak up pressure. Alan Smith and Michael Bridges had been playfully arguing over who would get to swap shirts with Rivaldo in the build-up to the game and the latter would have harmed his chances when he committed a strong foul on the Brazilian a few minutes into the game which required treatment. Barcelona soon began to take control of possession and proceedings and no sooner had Rivaldo returned to the field after his treatment was he scythed down again, this time by Olivier Dacourt. The world player of the year would have his revenge on nine minutes. He received the ball just inside the Leeds half and a deft first touch eliminated Dacourt and then played a pass through to Patrick Kluivert. Dacourt had recovered to tackle the Dutchman, but the ball found its way to Barcelona winger Simao on the wide right. Simao played into Rivaldo who had continued his run into the Leeds penalty area, another neat touch got him away from Michael Duberry who had come sliding in to block a shot but instead, Rivaldo cut inside and finished left-footed into Nigel Martyn's left-hand post. Barcelona doubled their lead ten minutes later when Frank De Boer was presented with a free-kick 30 yards from goal after Dacourt had again fouled Rivaldo. De Boer's effort was delicious and curled directly past Martyn's outstretched arms into the top left corner. The first signs of frustration crept into Leeds shortly before half-time when Danny Mills was booked for a high, studs' first challenge on Simao. Upon the restart of the second-half Leeds had enjoyed a good spell of possession which culminated in working the ball out wide to Bridges in the Barcelona area. His lofted cross evaded everyone and found Ian Harte unmarked from six yards, but he could only drive his shot into goalkeeper Richard Dutruel. A golden opportunity to half the arrears and get back into the game was spurned. As the half wore on O'Leary's fears about a mismatch were ever more realised. Smith let his frustration show with Leeds's inability to get into the game midway through the half and was booked for a heavy challenge on Phillip Cocu which forced him to leave the field. To replace him the hosts were able to bring on their expensive new signing Emmanuel Petit to freshen up their midfield whilst, in contrast, Leeds could only reply by sending on un-renowned academy player - Tony Hackworth, displaying the contrast in quality Leeds were up against in this competition and how they could ill afford to have such an extensive injury list. This was especially the case in Europe as the competition required clubs to name seven substitutes as opposed to the five then required in the Premier League. However, with fifteen minutes remaining Leeds at least had held Barcelona to a respectable scoreline, which was important should the final standings in the group be decided by goal difference. That small victory was extinguished however when Kluivert first converted a Simao cross with a simple finish on 75 minutes and added his second and Barcelona's fourth when he finished off a neat move with a clever turn to get away from Mills and set himself on to his favoured right foot to fire home. Leeds's miserable night was completed when Lucas Radebe and Michael Duberry clashed heads as they both challenged for the latter's original loose header. Radebe needed extensive treatment on the pitch before concerningly leaving the field on a stretcher and sporting a neck brace.

David O'Leary reflected on the defeat in his programme notes for the league game against Ipswich three days later. "Our visit to Barcelona was a salutary lesson for all of us. We have to hold our hands up and admit we were beaten by a better side – a team of wonderful individual players who on the night were too good for us; we cannot afford this number of injuries to key players and expect to do well at places like the Nou Camp".

Frank De Boer had felt underwhelmed by his opposition post-match stating, "We knew that Leeds normally plays in an aggressive way, trying to get the ball forward but against us they defended too deeply, dropping into their own half to make it easier for us. I was just not impressed by any of their players. We overwhelmed them. Maybe they will be tougher to beat on their own ground but here at the Camp Nou they were too naïve" was the Dutchman's frank assessment of United.

Although asking for a young, injury-depleted team to get a result against a star-studded Barcelona at Camp Nou on their own patch was a tough ask, it was a disappointing night and start to United's European campaign coupled with the concerning injury to Radebe. It was a classic case of men against boys and Leeds in fairness had shown up on their Champions League debut looking like uninvited guests at a party wearing the wrong dress code. The newspapers were no less kind. *The Independent* called it "a torrid initiation" whilst the *BBC* described the game "a painful lesson" for the Yorkshiremen. On this showing, Leeds's stay in the competition was going to be a fleeting one and the next game in the group wouldn't be any easier as they prepared to welcome (then) five-time European Champions AC Milan to Elland Road.

Singing in the Rain

UEFA Champions League, 1st Group Phase. Matchday Two

Vs AC Milan (Home)

Boos ringed around Elland Road after Leeds United suffered a second straight home defeat to a newly promoted side this time, 2-1 to Ipswich Town just days after the thrashing at the Nou Camp. The defeat meant Leeds had only picked up one point from an available nine in the league against favourable opposition in Manchester City, Coventry City, and Ipswich leaving them already adrift from the top of the Premier League table. After the heavy defeat at the Nou Camp Leeds were readying to welcome Italian giants AC Milan to Elland Road but knowing that a defeat would already make progression from the Champions League an improbable task.

The list of absentees from injuries was still extensive, now counting at seven, and was costing O'Leary who was growing increasingly agitated especially when news came that Mark Viduka – who was expected to report back to Thorp Arch after it was no longer possible for Australia to progress to the next round of the Olympic tournament – was told he had to fulfil his country's last fixture in the competition. Viduka was brought for these big nights and yet again was unavailable at a time when his club needed him. In his programme notes for the game, O'Leary conceded that he feels he had "a strong team but not a strong squad" and that he and his team were experiencing the first real blip in his two years in charge to date. Chairman Peter Ridsdale also used the platform of his programme column to voice his dissatisfaction at the "short memories" of supporters who had been disgruntled over recent form and reinforced the club's transfer policy of not spending their way out of trouble even though there was a transfer war chest at O'Leary's disposal.

Assistant manager Eddie Gary later revealed in his autobiography that an in-house team meeting took place in the away dressing room down in the bowels of Camp Nou after the Barcelona game where the management team sat the players down and talked about their approach to European football and what was needed. "The main part of the talk concerned the importance of believing in themselves and not allowing teams to walk all over them. One of the common denominators about the leading European Cup teams is that they all have strikers who can get goals out of nothing, and David and I tried to make the players realise that sitting back and allowing them to come on to us was tantamount to soccer suicide", Gray wrote.

***

Like Barcelona, Leeds United's forays into Europe in the 1960s and 70s meant they had history and unfinished business with AC Milan too. The two teams met in the 1973 European Cup Winners Cup final held in Thessaloniki, Greece. The game was won by Milan 1-0 but in a very controversial fashion. Mick Jones was absent from the game but came into the Leeds dressing room pre-match and warned his teammates that he had seen the Greek referee Christos Michas talking to representatives of Milan and that winning the game was going to be very difficult. Leeds fell behind to a Luciano Chiagrugi free-kick on five minutes but despite dominating the game, they couldn't find a way through and had several penalty claims dismissed. The unjust events of the match incensed Norman Hunter who was sent off for a challenge somewhat typical of the late Leeds legend. So obvious was the biasedness from Michas that the local Greek supporters cheered for Leeds and jeered and threw missiles at Milan whilst they paraded the trophy on their lap of honour. UEFA later banned Michas for life due to match-fixing, although this particular match was never investigated. Leeds had attempted to get the match replayed but were denied. In 2009 MEP for Yorkshire and the Humber Richard Corbett campaigned a petition that reached 15,000 signatures for UEFA to award Leeds United the title and the medals awarded to the Leeds United team of that night but again the claims were unsuccessful. The late great Hunter later commented that the odds were stacked against Leeds when he claimed, "I honestly don't think we were ever going to score that night because if we had netted a legitimate goal the referee would have chalked it off".

1973 aside, AC Milan are one of the most illustrious sides in European football. In 2000 they boasted five European cups (now seven), only second to Real Madrid, and had most recently won the competition in 1994 under Fabio Capello when they defeated Barcelona 4-0 in the final. The current crop had finished an underwhelming third in Serie A in 1999/00 behind Lazio and Juventus and thus had to navigate a qualifying round to reach the group stage, where they beat Croatians Dynamo Zagreb 6-1 on aggregate. They did have an extremely talented side with stalwarts Paulo Maldini, Demetrio Albertini, Alessandro Costacurta, and Oliver Bierhoff and were fronted by young Ukrainian marksman Andriy Shevchenko. Shevchenko won the Golden Boot in Serie A the previous season with 24 goals in 32 appearances. He had caught the eye in the Champions League two years earlier where he netted 11 goals for his native side Dynamo Kyiv on his way to becoming the competition's top scorer that season. Milan - managed by Alberto Zaccheroni – where yet to kick off their league campaign even in the middle of September. The Serie A scheduled to kick off on October 1st due to the Olympics tournament (a schedule that helped Italian teams domestically that had lost players to the games such as Leeds with Viduka). They had prepared for their opening Champions Leagues games with a friendly against Roma which they drew 2-2 and eased their way into the Champions League with a 4-1 win over Besiktas which rooted Leeds to the bottom of Group H. Milan was looking for a much-improved performance in Europe this campaign after finishing bottom of their group the previous season and Shevchenko likened the challenge as repaying a debt to the fans and the club.

An arduous task awaited United on the pitch, but one was also forced upon the stadium manager Harry Stokey, and his team as they prepared to get Elland Road Champions League ready. With the quick turnaround after the Ipswich game on Saturday afternoon to welcoming Milan on Tuesday evening, Stokey and his team of over 100 people had less than 48 hours to transform the stadium to meet UEFA's regulations. The operation included removing any traces of the normal advertising boards and replacing them with UEFA's partners and branding, installing media facilities for 100 extra written journalists and 27 groups of five-man crews of media. In addition, areas were created for temporary TV studios and interview rooms. The operation cost around £200,000 but most unfortunate was that taller advertisement boards resulted in the loss of the bottom rows of seating in each stand therefore reducing the capacity allowed for the games meaning fans missed out on tickets that were already like gold dust to get hold of and some season ticket holders were forced to make way to alternative seating.

Milan boss Alberto Zaccheroni was aware of Leeds's injury woes and was pleased he wouldn't have to plan for a way to thwart Harry Kewell whom he had admired but admitted somewhat condescendingly that it could still be a difficult game for the Italians "I respect Leeds. They compete very well. They are a threat at home and can lift their game against the big sides" he stated.

Milan was given a very Yorkshire welcome as the rain hammered down on Elland Road on this Tuesday evening under the lights. Leeds was able to welcome back Erik Bakke to the starting line-up and Dominic Matteo was ready for his debut for the club albeit out of position on the wide left to add balance to the team. O'Leary had been warned against forcing the pair back too early after injury but the crisis with seven players missing necessitated that they played. The pair had struck up a good friendship since Matteo's arrival and were now sharing a pitch after sharing a sofa to watch the past two Champions League matches. However, after Radebe's injury at Camp Nou, O'Leary was forced into naming a makeshift centre-back partnership of Danny Mills and Michael Duberry to thwart Shevchenko and Bierhoff.

Milan came closest to opening the scoring when Ian Harte had dwelt on the ball for too long and allowed Thomas Helveg a shot on goal that hit the side netting. The Elland Road crowd, despite their team's poor run of form and the daunting opposition in front of them, were in fine voice and Alan Smith had increased the intensity of the game as he hassled Milan and wouldn't let their defence breathe when on the ball. The conditions and the tempo of the game made for an atmosphere akin to an FA Cup tie with the smell of an upset in the air. Leeds's first chance of the game came as Olivier Dacourt caught Albertini in possession and played the ball out wide to Matteo who crossed into Smith. Brazillian goalkeeper Dida came out to punch the ball away uncertainly only as far as Bakke whose shot was parried by Dida and cleared before Michael Bridges could tap home. Leeds came close again shortly after, a free-kick exchange between Dacourt and Lee Bowyer resulted in Bakke just getting underneath his header which went over the bar from six yards. The hosts were enjoying a good first-half spell and created chances with Gary Kelly (the oldest outfield player for Leeds at 26) marauding forward. Leeds again came close with headers from Matteo and Bridges.

The rain continued to lash down but the 35,398 crowd were warmed by the spirited first-half performance from the Whites. Their endeavour continued into the second half - Dacourt was putting in a demanding performance at the heart of midfield and Bowyer was driving Leeds forward at every opportunity. As Milan struggled with the conditions and intensity their frustration grew and this showed when Argentina international Guly dived inside the Leeds penalty area when feeling the slightest of contact of Dacourt's left leg, but his claims were dismissed by Austrian referee Gunter Benko. Similarly, shortly after Smith went down in the area after a challenge but his protests for a spot kick were also correctly waved away. Smith at just 19 years of age was given his marker - the legendary Paulo Maldini, twelve years his senior – a torrid time, and the Italian was booked when he resorted to pulling Smith's shirt as he passed him when out of position. Milan did manage to grow into the second half, however. A breakaway resulted in Shevchenko blasting a shot over the bar and minutes later he forced Nigel Martyn into a fingertip save to deny him with the visitor's first shot on target. The Ukrainian was then again denied by Martyn after Bierhoff had played him in on the right but saw his shot at the near post saved.

As the game entered its final minute of regulation time and with the two sides arguably happy to take a point and take refuge in the warmth of the dressing rooms, Bakke played a pass into Bowyer in midfield. Bowyer had space to drive into and could hear the shouts of Kelly to "run at them". Instead, Bowyer took a touch into space and let fly a shot that was on target but not looking like it should trouble Dida in the Milan goal. As Dida went to claim the ball, he lost grip of his initial catch and fumbled the wet, greasy ball as it passed the goal line and with it himself as he tried to rectify his error. Elland Road had erupted. It was a fortuitous goal but a welcome and deserved one on the night. Bowyer reeled away one arm outstretched alas Alan Shearer and was mobbed by his teammates. Clive Tyldesley, commentating for ITV captured the mood of the club perfectly with his closing line, "booed off on Saturday, cheered to the rafters tonight". Paulo Maldini was booked in the game for attempting to pull Alan Smith's shirt off his back. He eventually got it as he and Smith swapped shirts. It was a sign of respect that during the game Leeds simply did not afford Milan, to preach what they were taught in the Nou Camp dressing room a week previously. So perplexed was Maldini with the energy and dynamism the Leeds players had shown on the night, O'Leary later revealed an exchange between him and the Milan legend to *The Athletic*. "I had played against Paolo Maldini in the past. He came up to me at half-time and said, 'David what are you feeding your players on? They're mad the way they charge around'".

Match winner Bowyer reflected on his teammate's resilience after the Barcelona defeat. "When we lost in Barcelona we gave them too much respect, but we set about AC Milan from the start. We were determined not to let them dominate us on our own patch and we deserved the win. The Champions League was new to us when we played Barcelona and we gave them too much room, but we didn't make that mistake against Milan".

O'Leary was jubilant with the victory but cautious not to get ahead of himself with this one result. "I just love beating the Italians because I have great admiration for them, and you know you are beating the top of the tree. This was my biggest game to date so it is definitely the biggest result of my managerial career" he stated before adding "but I'm sure if we lose to Besiktas next week then people will probably start saying we are a bad team again".

Not only had Leeds gained their first points on the board in Group H, coupled with Besiktas's shock 3-0 victory over Barcelona all four teams were tied on three points each ahead of Leeds's double-header with Besiktas.

Besiktas – A Record Equalling Victory and an Unwanted Return to Istanbul

UEFA Champions League, Group H, Matchdays 3 and 4.

Vs Besiktas (Home & Away)

If there was excitement and satisfaction in the Leeds United camp after being drawn alongside Barcelona and AC Milan it was soon dilated once the ball from Pot 4 was picked out and revealed to complete Group H. Being grouped with the Turkish side Besiktas was a nightmare scenario everyone knew was possible but had hoped wouldn't come to fruition. The prospect of returning to Istanbul, just four months after the atrocities that occurred at the city centre's Taksim Square, which cost the lives of fans Kevin Speight (40) and Christopher Loftus (37), was an ordeal that no one of a Leeds United persuasion wanted. A return to the Turkish capital was the least desired travel destination for not only Leeds fans but for a city united in grief and anger. It was also an unwanted scenario for O'Leary's young squad who would be forced to return to the city where most of them had played in front of an intensely intimidating crowd at the Ali Sami Yen Stadium and were chaperoned from the tunnel by riot police and guarded by shields on to the pitch.

Yet Leeds United's traveling hoards wherever they go would not be deterred, especially as this was one of possibly only three opportunities to follow their team in the Champions League. Thankfully, it became clear from the start that dealings with Besiktas were a lot more pleasant than their experiences with Galatasaray. For example, Besiktas's president Sirdar Bidgili came to England of his own accord to meet the directors of Leeds United, and an agreement was made for only 250 away fans to be allocated tickets for each game to limit the possibility of any potential trouble. O'Leary had initially urged Leeds United fans not to travel to the away game but eventually, chairman Peter Ridsdale had contacted the families of Speight and Loftus for their opinion and blessing for supporters to travel to Turkey if they so wished along with seeking advice from the Leeds United Supporters Club and West Yorkshire Police.

David O'Leary reflected in his book *Leeds United on Trial* how the logistics of being paired with Besiktas was of primary concern before any footballing matters could be considered. "Immediately after the Champions League pairings were announced, rather than savouring the trips to Milan and Barcelona we had to prioritise the management and security of the games against Besiktas. It was of paramount importance that Leeds fans did not head to Istanbul in a spirit of revenge and we were equally concerned about policing Elland Road if there was a massive influx of Turkish fans for the home game, which was scheduled first", wrote the Leeds boss. "I was assured by the Leeds officials who discussed the high-risk security situation with the Turks that thankfully Besiktas seemed to be a very different club from Galatasaray. Their approach was to try to build bridges and nullify any potential hatred, whereas Galatasaray's attitude had been to whip up ill feelings to produce a powder-keg atmosphere that suited them and intimidated visitors".

Leeds United Chairman Ridsdale and Besiktas Club President Bilgili released a joint statement following the draw. "We see this as an opportunity for everyone connected with football to look forward and demonstrate that the game can be fulfilled in safety and in the right sporting spirit".

As if preparing to host a Champions League fixture wasn't demanding enough, the preparations for the visit of Besiktas were plunged into the measures of a high-security event rather than the mere event of a football match. UEFA officials had made plans immediately after the draw to visit Elland Road and discuss safety issues with the Leeds board. Leeds United teamed up quickly and productively with West Yorkshire Police to ensure the occasion would pass without incident. Leeds shared the additional financial strain to police the match and security was organised to a level in which Elland Road – despite its previous notoriety for crowd violence in the 1970s and 80s – had ever seen. Elland Road Stadium manager Harry Stokey said "We will have over 600 stewards on duty while the police will have an enormous presence outside the stadium and around 150 officers inside. To give you some scale of this, that compares to around 90 police who are usually in the stadium for a match against Manchester United". Leeds's operations director David Spencer was wary that the game had the potential for unsavoury scenes despite the level of security organised. He stated "no matter how much planning goes into it, there is still the possibility of individual nutters causing a problem. But we will do our best to isolate any troublemakers. We would hope all our Turkish visitors will feel welcome and comfortable, and we can play a match in the true spirit of football".

***

Meanwhile, between the European encounters with Milan and Besiktas, Leeds couldn't build on their victory over Milan when they returned to Premier League action over the weekend as they continued their stumbling start to the domestic season with a 1-1 draw away to 10-man Derby County. Derby was down to ten after 35 minutes when Horacio Carbonari was shown red immediately after Ian Harte had put the Whites ahead. However, Leeds couldn't build on their advantage and were stung by Georgi Kinkladze's 75th-minute equaliser which extended United's winless league run to four matches.

The Group H standings made for intriguing reading after each team was tied on three points apiece after two rounds of games. As Leeds prepared for a double-header against Besiktas, likewise Barcelona and Milan were doing the same. Despite Besiktas's impressive 3-0 victory over Barcelona last time out, Leeds knew they had a golden opportunity to collect points from the lowest seeds in the group whilst the two favourites would be dropping points against each other and that the table had the potential to make for pretty reading for Leeds after the final whistle was blown on Matchday 4. It seemed like a group-defining few weeks for the four teams.

***

There had been a steady rise in Turkish football over the 1990s crossing into the new millennium. Galatasaray went on to defeat Arsenal in the final of the UEFA Cup after beating Leeds in the semi-final and the Turkish national team had made it to the Quarter-Finals of Euro 2000 a couple of months earlier - one stage further than England managed and two years later they would go one further and reach the semi-finals of the 2002 World Cup in South Korea and Japan. Besiktas were, and still are widely considered to be Turkey's third club, after Istanbul neighbours Galatasaray and Fenerbahçe. They were originally formed as a gymnastics club in 1903 and British football fans may have recognised them from a spell a young Les Ferdinand had at the club in the late eighties and were recently managed by John Toshack before he made his move to Real Madrid. English coach Gordon Milne had also led the club to three successive league titles in the early 1990s. They had reached the Champions League group stage after finishing as runners-up in the Turkish Süper Lig in 1999/00 and defeated Levski Sofia and then Lokomotiv Moscow in qualifying. Going into the game, Besiktas, like Leeds themselves, had experienced contrasting results against the two group heavyweights. They fell to a 4-1 defeat to AC Milan at the San Siro on opening night before recovering to defeat Barcelona 3-0 at home with Armet Dursan a two-goal hero for the 'Black Eagles'.

Before the game, Ridsdale had used his programme notes to publicly praise the president and directors of the Turkish club for the way they have handled the difficult situation of the clubs being paired together, despite the blame and ignition of the controversy laying away from their club. "It is therefore with genuine feelings of friendship that we welcome everyone from Besiktas to the game", he wrote.

Going into Matchday 3 O'Leary had admitted that his side was ahead of schedule and that he would have settled for one point from the opening two games but here they were with three. In team news, Danny Mills came in to replace the injured Michael Duberry but the main topic of discussion regarded the involvement of United's new star striker Mark Viduka, who had returned from his exploits at the Sydney Olympics but had yet to score for his new club and his international duty absence had frustrated his manager and fans alike. There were sections of the media suggesting that O'Leary would drop the Aussie for the Champions League clash as a punishment for his absence and leaving an injury struck Leeds in the lurch, but these were claims that O'Leary admitted he "never considered for a moment". And so Viduka came in replacing Michael Bridges - who himself was yet to find the target in nine games in the season to date despite topping the scoring charts in the previous season. It had the feeling of a fresh start for Viduka and that this would be his real debut for Leeds United.

Besiktas took to the field carrying bouquets during the pre-match formalities which were then handed to Leeds fans in another public example of the truce between the two clubs. Besiktas were known for their employment of a counter-attacking style of play, but they were forced onto the back foot regardless by Leeds's aggressive attacking start from the opening whistle, camping themselves in the visitor's half. However, it was Besiktas that came closest to taking the lead. Slovakia international midfielder Miroslav Karhan unleashed a strong shot from 30 yards out which just brushed wide of Nigel Martyn's goal. However, from the resultant goal kick, Leeds themselves engineered a move that resulted in the first goal of the night. Ian Harte had made an overlapping run wide on the left and when played in he produced a trademark left-footed pearl of a cross in front of the face of goal which at first evaded Erik Bakke at the front post but met Lee Bowyer for a simple finish from close range and the floodgates were opened after just seven minutes. Shortly after, the man in the spotlight, Viduka, had run onto a looped ball over the top of the defence by his striking partner Alan Smith and was in acres of space and looked certain to open his scoring account in a White shirt but his effort was saved by Nigerian international goalkeeper Ike Shorunmu onto the crossbar. The disappointment of the missed effort didn't last for long though and Viduka finally scored his maiden goal for the club converting a powerful downwards header before gleefully sliding on his knees, arms outstretched in front of the West Stand in what is now an iconic image for Leeds fans. Viduka, buoyant from his goal tried his luck again ten minutes later but again found his shot saved and out for a corner. From the resultant corner Matteo had turned cleverly in the six-yard box to fire home and Leeds were holding an unassailable 3-0 lead with less than a quarter of the match played. Leeds was playing with a youthful tenacity that they had shown many times during

O'Leary's reign to date but was evading them in the Premier League in the opening weeks of the season. They again came close to increasing their lead before half-time again through Matteo and then the notoriously goal-shy Lucas Radebe had fancied his chances at a long-range effort that blazed over the bar - such was United's confidence.

Leeds did however experience a brief poor period in the second half perhaps born out of complacency. Martyn was called upon for the first time in the game when Ahmet Dursan was played in behind the Leeds defence but saved his effort with an outstretched right boot and shortly after Leeds were again let off when Umit Bozkurt found himself in a promising position only to blast his effort into the side netting.

Leeds though, backed by a vociferous Elland Road crowd reasserted themselves and put the game to bed. Viduka had a shot saved and parried and as he contemplated another shot whilst surrounded by three Besiktas defenders he saw the unmarked run of Bakke who despite slipping as he struck the ball, managed to keep it on target for 4-0.

With the game tied up, frustrations got the better of Besiktas with still twenty minutes to go. Radebe, who had only just returned from that concerning injury at the Nou Camp had stayed down after making a tackle in the centre of the pitch. Markus Munch of Besiktas had ignored the pleas of the Leeds players and supporters to kick the ball out of play, as was his prerogative. But once Mills had intercepted Munch's attack and the ball went out of play for a corner, Gary Kelly let Munch know what he thought of his ignorance of Radebe's injury sparking the only unsavoury incident of the evening. Mills chose to join in with the argument as Kelly was pulled away by Martyn when Pascal Nouma struck Mills with his forearm. The Frenchman had a tendency for controversy in his career and had attracted a lot of attention at the time for an incident that took place in an Istanbul nightclub. He was instantly removed from the action by his coach Nevio Scala before the referee could send him off, cleverly leaving Besiktas with a full complement of players although Nouma was not completely out of jail yet.

Darren Huckerby was brought on with ten minutes to go replacing Smith who was guilty of the only negative of the evening from a Leeds perspective as he picked up his third booking of the European campaign and would therefore be suspended for the return trip to Istanbul. Huckerby however had made the most of a rare appearance when he made it 5-0 as the game entered past the ninety-minute mark. A Lee Bowyer corner was met by an unchallenged free header for Harte and the ball dropped to Huckerby, who facing away from goal, controlled, and turned goalward in one motion and converted. This goal would later form part of a unique collection as he became the only player to have scored in all top four divisions of English football and the Champions League. It turned out to be his final goal for Leeds though and was transferred to Manchester City for £3.38 million three months later.

Bowyer drew praise from his manager for his display in this match. According to O'Leary, the midfielder had "epitomised our approach, and the fact that he opened and closed the scoring was a fitting tribute to his industry". Bowyer, tireless as ever, had won the ball in his half and drove forwards before laying the ball out wide to Huckerby. Huckerby with the adrenaline of his goal moments earlier still running through his veins, himself drove into the Besiktas penalty area before sliding the ball across the face of the goal where it was met by Bowyer who had continued his run for an almost carbon copy of the first goal to neatly bookend the game.

Dominic Matteo later reflected on this evening as the night that "turned out to be the moment people started to sit up and take notice of Leeds United. And I am not exaggerating when I say we could have scored ten", he wrote in his autobiography.

After the initial pressure put on him before the game, Viduka was one of the stars of the night. He stated, "This is one of the best team performances I have ever been involved in. To score six goals in the Champions League is special for any team. I have to say it is a big relief now that I have got my first goal for Leeds. Hopefully, there will be plenty more to follow".

The manager was full of praise for his team's performance. "These nights don't come around very often, and I thought we were marvellous. Our movement, pace, and passing set the tone right from the start. We scored some beautiful goals, and I am starting to enjoy the Champions League". Matteo also later revealed that the young Leeds players took full advantage of being the toast of the city with a night out in the Majestyk nightclub in Leeds city Centre and lapped up the offers of free drinks and female attention.

Importantly, after all the fret about the visit of a side from Istanbul so soon after the tragic events of the previous April, the game had passed by without incident. The margin of victory equalled the Champions League record at the time. Ironically, Besiktas were the unlucky team when that record was beaten again on English soil in 2007-08 when they lost 8-0 to Liverpool at Anfield. The result was also Leeds's biggest home victory for 16 years since an identical scoreline in a Second Division game versus Oldham Athletic in 1984. However, this was on the biggest stage and Leeds United had now truly announced their arrival. Elsewhere in the group Milan overcame Barcelona 2-0 and coupled with United's margin of victory meant they stood proudly on top of Group H at the halfway stage. From rock bottom with a goal difference of -4 to group leaders with a positive goal difference of +3 in just two games. Alan Smith summed up the feeling by talking to ITV after the game. "No one would have thought that (we would be top of the group) when we went to Barcelona and got beat 4-0 but that's the spirit of this club". It had been some turnaround.

***

Leeds sat proudly at the summit of Group H for three weeks whilst the Champions League hit the pause button halfway through the first group phase to accommodate the international break, which would turn out to be seismic for English football. England had lost their opening game of qualifying for the 2002 World Cup, 1-0 to arch-nemesis Germany in which was the last ever game to be played under the Twin Towers of the original Wembley Stadium. Kevin Keegan immediately quit as manager in the toilets after the game. Despite his Irish nationality (although born in London), David O'Leary was suggested by sections of the media to be Keegan's successor although apparently, he was never considered. However, that wouldn't have been due to his nationality as would later appear in due course with a shortage of successful and promising home-grown coaches in the Premier League. Keegan would temporarily be replaced by Leeds's title-winning maestro Howard Wilkinson as he oversaw an underwhelming 0-0 draw away to Finland. The England squad was not represented by United pair Jonathan Woodgate and Lee Bowyer however due to their suspension by The Football Association until the outcome of their ongoing court case would be decided. Woodgate had already made his England debut in June 1999 but had yet to add to this initial cap (although would end his career with eight caps). For Bowyer, this must have been a frustrating time for his international aspirations, in the form of his life but unavailable for selection for non-footballing reasons. He would have to wait until September 2002 for his first and only appearance for the Three Lions in a 1-1 friendly draw with Portugal at Villa Park. Elsewhere, Alan Smith scored but then was sent off playing for England's U21 after retaliating to a foul in a game against Finland. He was already suspended for his club's upcoming Champions League visit to Besiktas, and this was a further example of the youngster's overzealousness harming his development in the early years of his career.

The international break sandwiched two home victories for Leeds as they got their Premier League campaign back on track. Fresh from their 6-0 victory over Besiktas, they came out victorious in an exhilarating 4-3 victory over George Graham's Tottenham Hotspur, ironically two years to the day that he ditched West Yorkshire for North London. Upon returning to domestic action after the break, Leeds brushed past Charlton Athletic 3-1. Mark Viduka's goal against Besiktas had proved the catalyst for better things as he netted a brace in each of the two games. The Charlton victory didn't come without problems though as attention turned to the resumption of European competition. The Elland Road club shop was already selling VHS copies for the emphatic 6-0 triumph, but they would be traveling to Turkey without two key players. Oliver Dacourt was injured and replaced by Jacob Burns who was signed in the summer as a backup player more than one who would make a difference and would find himself involved in some of the club's most illustrious games in the coming weeks. Perhaps more concerningly though was the injury to goalkeeper Nigel Martyn who had his run of 68 consecutive appearances curtailed when he was forced out of action mid-game. He was replaced by promising England U21 international Paul Robinson on the eve of his 21st birthday. Robinson's last game came nearly two seasons previously after making his debut by keeping a clean sheet in a 0-0 home draw with Chelsea two years prior. Although Robinson was highly rated it was a concern for Leeds to be without their first-choice goalkeeper and most experienced player as they entered a key period in both the league and in Europe.

***

For the commencement of the Champions League, Leeds made their much talked about return to Istanbul and the unusual but pleasant setting off the Inonu stadium. Much unlike the vast but compact steep stands of the Camp Nou and San Siro, the Inonu stadium was an oval structure with uncovered stands separated from the pitch by an athletics track. It sat surrounded by trees and grass on the foot of hills leading to the famous Bosporus River which separates the European and Asian sections of Istanbul. It was the setting for Barcelona's 3-0 humiliation a month earlier.

The increased security and the absence of any Besiktas supporters had ensured that the meeting of the sides at Elland Road had passed without major incident but it was always the return of Leeds United to Istanbul that caused the most concern. Dominic Matteo, newly signed wasn't at the club for the last visit to Istanbul but had reflected in his autobiography the mood of his teammates returning to the scene of such difficult memories. "I could tell the lads had been badly affected by what had happened and, for some, it was an emotional experience to go back so soon". He also claimed how their hotel rooms were guarded by armed guards throughout their stay. "It was quite unnerving, and I remember looking at one of the policemen on our floor who had a machine gun and thinking, 'What is this all about? We are footballers, not the president of some country", Matteo said.

Leeds United's players, fans, and media arrived at Istanbul airport to be greeted by the sight of over a hundred armed police officers. Unlike Besiktas at the Elland Road match, a select few hundred Leeds fans had made the trip to support their team after being given the blessing of the families of Kevin Speight and Christopher Loftus. Yorkshire Television was televising the game live despite it not being the chosen networked game by ITV so that fans would be able to stay at home and watch the game. The fans that did travel were unable to make a holiday or trip of the occasion however as travel was restricted to a day return package organised by the club. Fans were ferried from the airport along the Bosphorus river for a two-hour journey arriving just 20 minutes before kick-off to keep them off the streets for security reasons. Leeds fans on the boat displayed their humour with a banner stating "LUFSea"

Despite the increased security in place and the co-operative measures put in place between the two clubs, the evening unfortunately didn't pass without incident. The coach carrying members of the press covering the game for Leeds United was pelted with stones as it approached the stadium. An intimidating atmosphere was brewing among the Besiktas supporters at the Inonu stadium, although it should be argued that this is normally the case for visitors to Istanbul teams for European clashes and was perhaps not fabricated just for Leeds United's arrival.

With Martyn ruled out, Robinson was plunged into the deep for only a seventh senior appearance. Besiktas were dealt a setback with the retrospective suspension of Pascal Nouma following his actions in the Elland Road meeting. Despite his fury at being substituted immediately after the incident, throwing his shirt at the team's bench in disgust, he at least thought he had escaped the punishment of a red card and a suspension, but UEFA had suspended him for three games for striking Danny Mills. Besiktas's decision to appeal the ban backfired on them however when UEFA duly extended the ban to four games. Nouma's frustrations would not have tempered either after the final whistle of the first game, provoked by comments made by his former Lens team-mate Oliver Dacourt during the game. "I asked him if he thought we were playing tennis. Six-love, first set. I told him it would be game, set, and match to Leeds in Turkey", Dacourt teased.

As Martyn and Dacourt were added to the extensive injury list, Leeds was at least boosted by the return to fitness of Jonathan Woodgate who had only managed two full games in the season to date. Woodgate was under no illusions that the away game would be a very different occasion to the one enjoyed in the home game. "Besiktas are a very good team, as they showed by beating Barcelona 3-0 the week before we played them. It will be a different game over in Istanbul and I just hope I can be involved", he said.

David O'Leary also pleaded for calm from supporters as excitement grew over what the team could achieve. "I know some people have already pencilled us into the UEFA Champions League second stage after our wins over AC Milan and Besiktas, but we are keeping a much more balanced view. We know that to get a win in Istanbul is going to be very difficult, and even if we manage that, there is still the small matter of taking something from Barcelona and/or Milan. It's far from a done deal but we've put ourselves into a good position and we're looking forward to trying to finish the job", was his cautioning.

Despite the 20,000 in attendance being far short of the stadium's capacity the atmosphere was white hot as the teams took the field. Michael Bridges came in for the suspended Alan Smith for what would turn out to be a fateful night for the 21-year-old. Elsewhere Jonathan Woodgate did make the side for his first Champions League appearance and Burns continued to deputise for the injured Dacourt.

It was overall a game of few chances, and a 0-0 draw was perhaps overdue to a group that had already seen 21 goals before kick-off. The best chance of the game fell the way of the visitors in the first half. A wide free-kick on the left delivered by Bowyer found Erik Bakke at the back post after Besiktas displayed some poor man marking as they did in the first meeting, but Ike Shorumu was equal to the Norwegians effort from just five yards out and a golden opportunity to take the lead was spurned.

In an evening that had the potential to turn sour, the worse incident of the evening from a Leeds perspective came midway through the first half when an innocuous challenge had left Bridges in a heap on the floor, which was bemoaned by Besiktas players who were not to know the extent of the injury.

A bottle was hurled from the crowd at Bridges as he left the field on a stretcher. It was a desperately unfortunate knee injury for the youngster who would never score another goal for Leeds, and despite forging a decent career at several clubs including a later move to his (near) hometown club Newcastle United, he would never recover enough to fulfil his career's initial promise.

Bakke's early chance was as close as Leeds would get although Viduka looked to have continued his fine goal-scoring form with a volley from an acute angle which was struck into the side netting.

Besiktas were looking to rectify their heavy defeat at Elland Road in front of their home supporters and were the protagonists in the game without ever really troubling the youngster Robinson in the Leeds goal with a string of shots off target and whatever he did have to deal with he did well.

A 0-0 draw may have seemed underwhelming to the uninitiated considering they had beaten these same opponents 6-0 in their last European game, but this was a very mature performance from a very young team in intimidating surroundings and the point gained kept Leeds in control of their own destiny in the group. The team fielded by O'Leary was one of the youngest ever to represent Leeds United with an average age of 22. All the more impressive for the fact that this was an evening that even a group of hardened professionals would find difficult to negotiate.

Post-match, Robinson drew individual praise from O'Leary. The Leeds boss admitted this wasn't the type of game he would have liked to bring him in for and would have preferred for different circumstances. However, Robinson had always been highly rated by all at Leeds United to be Nigel Martyn's long-term successor which he eventually was in 2002 before going on to represent England as first-choice goalkeeper in the 2006 World Cup. The young stopper was humble in his comments post-match praising his defence. "It wasn't a difficult evening from my point of view because I was very well protected by Kells, Hartey, Woody, and Millsy. They all played very well – as they have done for the last few weeks", Robinson said.

O'Leary was also delighted to have gained a "valuable" point and pointed to a third consecutive clean sheet in the competition, but his comments pointed to an air of regret they couldn't win the game. Reflecting on his programme notes a week later he stated, "We know we can play better than we did against Besiktas, but I was delighted with the players' attitude and application. It was a difficult situation. The Turks were obviously keen to wipe out the memory of the hammering we gave them (at Elland Road), and they are no slouches on their own ground – you mustn't forget that they beat Barcelona 3-0 there".

O'Leary had to face some strange comments from the Turkish media after the game. One journalist asked him: "Why did you come to Turkey? To fight or to play in a game?" which was unusual as the game was hardly a dirty affair. After another journalist had questioned if O'Leary had purposely instructed his substitutes to warm up in front of the Besiktas bench. "Was it done on purpose to distract (Besiktas coach) Mr Scala's concentration?". By this point, a tired and unimpressed O'Leary had had enough. "I have answered your questions politely but if you won't ask me any proper football questions, I will move on to my good friends in the English press", he retorted.

Away from football, the two fixtures brought none of the potential major difficulties in terms of crowd control and the safety of supporters. "I was extremely grateful to the families of Christopher Loftus and Kevin Speight for their understanding in allowing us to take supporters with us – a decision I am relieved we made. I would also like to thank the president of Besiktas and everyone connected with his club for the way they made us feel both welcome and safe", Ridsdale quoted after the tie.

On the pitch – the point gained was perceived as a valuable one. Matchdays 3 and 4 of Group H threatened to be group-defining and Leeds had come out of them flying high and on the brink of progression to the second group phase. Whilst Leeds and Besiktas played out a goalless draw, Milan and Barcelona shared the goals in a six-goal thriller drawing 3-3 at the San Siro, with World Footballer of the Year Rivaldo netting a hat-trick. Leeds wasn't home and dry yet however as they had the small matter of another round of games against the two giants of the group. They did though know that a famous Elland Road win over Barcelona a week later would see them through with a game to spare.

Last Minute Heartbreak

Barcelona (Home)

UEFA Champions League, 1st Group Phase, Matchday 5

Perhaps the biggest game staged at Elland Road in its history of over a century was the European Cup Semi-Final in 1975 when Leeds United welcomed Barcelona - captained by the immortal Johan Cruyff. The talented team had a large Dutch flavour, almost a year on from the Netherlands' 1974 World Cup campaign - where they lost out in the final to hosts West Germany but won the hearts of football purists with their 'Total Football' philosophy. In addition to Cruyff the Barcelona team that rocked up to West Yorkshire that spring included other notable Dutch names from the World Cup such as midfielder John Neeskens and up until the previous season were managed by the mastermind behind 'Total Football' - Rinus Michels. Billy Bremner and Allan Clarke scored either side of a Juan Manuel Asensi goal in front of 50,593 spectators to give Leeds a first-leg advantage to take to Camp Nou for the second leg. Nearby Thackley in Bradford was an unlikely setting to see such stars, but the town's residents couldn't believe their luck as the Catalans chose Thackley Football Club as their training base for the game and welcomed locals to watch Cruyff and co be put through their paces. It was after this game that Cruyff heaped high praise indeed on United when he described their ability to keep possession. "If you give Leeds the ball, they will make you dance", he said. That quote is proudly printed on a wall inside an entrance to Elland Road today. He admired the Millenial Leeds side too as David O'Leary revealed to *The Athletic* in 2021. "I remember playing golf out in Girona with Johan Cruyff, great man, and he told me we were like 'football rock and roll'".

It could be argued that the 2000 edition of Barcelona visiting Elland Road was the next biggest game the club had staged. David O'Leary certainly thought so in his programme notes for the game. "Clubs don't come any bigger or richer than Barcelona, and this is sure to be one of the biggest games in Leeds United's history. It's certainly a symbol of just how far we have come in the last couple of years. These nights are special and the kind we shall talk about in years to come" he quoted.

The two clubs' fate in Europe had changed drastically since Barcelona's 4-0 win over the Whites on opening night. A 3-0 defeat to Besiktas alongside a 3-3 draw and 2-0 reverse to AC Milan meant the Catalans would be eliminated with defeat at Elland Road. In contrast, Leeds had since made a mockery of the so-called 'Group of Death' and were sitting proudly on top knowing that a memorable victory at Elland Road would secure their passage to the second group phase with a game to spare.

There were reasons for Leeds to be positive and confident going into the match. O'Leary publicly pointed out that Barcelona's recent form since the two sides last met had been questionable but warned that anyone tempted to think the Whites could enter the game as favourites to put that out of their minds, Barca may have had a few hiccups but they are a formidable side with about 30 individuals to call on, and if we can beat them tonight it will be a great, great result" the Leeds gaffer said. Both teams went into this game after weekend games against their biggest rivals as Barca came out on top in *El Classico* defeating Real Madrid 2-0 at Camp Nou whereas Leeds headed to Old Trafford to face foes Manchester United.

Barcelona were frequent visitors to England since the competition's rebranding and these visits were seldom fruitful for them. Their five previous visits had generated 25 goals including a 2-2 and 3-3 draws respectively at Manchester United, a 3-2 defeat to Newcastle United, defeat to Chelsea at Stamford Bridge in the previous season, with their only victory coming at Wembley where they beat Arsenal (who were playing at the national stadium for their Champions League games in 1998-99 and 1999-00).

In addition, despite their *classico* win, there were reports of an unhappy Barcelona camp as they travelled north to England with rumours of dissenting voices from players towards under-fire new manager Lorenzo Serra Ferrer who had been promoted from within in the summer following the departure of Luis Van Gaal. These reports were not quashed by midfielder Phillip Cocu (who was playing the last time Leeds lost a European home game back in 1995 with PSV Eindhoven) in a pre-match interview. "It is inevitable that some players will feel frustrated when they don't play but we have to forget all about that when we play Leeds. We need a win". The risk of an early elimination from the Champions League was heaping further pressure from elsewhere on Serra Ferrer but he was not the only one singled out for criticism. World Player of the Year Rivaldo was also jeered by his home crowd in Barca's 2-0 defeat to Milan in the Champions League after a string of missed chances. It was just an off night for the Brazilian however as he had managed to score eight goals in his last eight appearances.

In the six days since the return to Istanbul, United had the small matter of a Roses derby against bitter rivals Manchester United. However, an almost unbelievable injury list contributed to a 3-0 reverse at Old Trafford. O'Leary justified the defeat with his mismatched team he put out quoting, "It is no disrespect to the lads who were out there to say we fielded a starting eleven that I never thought would begin a game this season. The size of the problem we faced is underlined by the 'team' we couldn't send out: Martyn, Mills, Radebe, Duberry, Harte, Bakke, Dacourt, Batty, Wilcox, Bridges and Kewell". In contrast, the Manchester United bench held an embarrassment of riches seating full internationals David Beckham, Ryan Giggs, Andy Cole, Wes Brown and Mark Bosnich. Despite half of his squad occupying the busy physio room at Thorp Arch training ground, O'Leary was optimistic his remaining troops could get the job done in the final two games of the group. "I'm still hopeful that we can get the points we need from the last two games to reach our goal of going into the second stage of the competition. To do so at the first attempt would be a marvellous achievement, like reaching our final", he stated.

The omens were looking promising for Leeds had never lost at home to a Spanish side with two wins and three draws in encounters with Real Zaragoza, Valencia and Barcelona and were unbeaten at home in ten European home games under O'Leary's stewardship. They could also call on a blossoming strike partnership of Mark Viduka and Alan Smith who had scored eight goals between them in the last five games with the latter available again after sitting out the Besiktas draw through suspension. Both spoke in the matchday programme about how they felt the team had learnt from their thrashing in Catalonia and how it would stand them in good stead for the game ahead. "I didn't think we were as bad in Barcelona as everyone seemed to make out. They scored two late goals, and we had a couple of chances in the second half which could have turned it round if they had gone in. We are looking for revenge tonight", Smith said.

Viduka looked forward to playing in front of a vociferous Elland Road crowd that he was beginning to win over after his false start to his Leeds career due to his Australia commitments at the Sydney Olympics. "No matter what happens, the experience that all of us have gained so far will prove important. It can only help the team's development. The fans help turn occasions like this one into unbelievable nights. You always want to do well in your home games, and I think the atmosphere is so good that it sometimes pulls us through", he said. He also praised his younger strike partner. "My partnership with Smithy has been working well and I hope that can continue".

***

On the back of their two previous home victories to date and the point earned in Istanbul, Leeds took to the field needing just two more points to qualify. A win would send them through to the second group stage with a game to spare and eliminate Barcelona in the process, so it was high stakes for both teams. Leeds without seven first-team regulars could at least recall Olivier Dacourt and Ian Harte to return to the starting line up in addition to Danny Mills, Erik Bakke, and Alan Smith who all passed late fitness tests. Barcelona themselves had a lengthy absentee list of their own, Emmanuel Petit, Pep Guardiola, Marc Overmars, and Patrick Kluivert were all unavailable, but their line up did include two youngsters who would become World Cup winners with Spain a decade later in centre-back Carles Puyol and midfielder Xavi Hernandez.

Leeds made a fast start to the game and quickly earned a free-kick in a dangerous position central to the goal after Puyol left a high foot on Dominic Matteo. The loud Elland Road crowd sang Harte's name in expectation as the free-kick specialist set his sights on goal. However, his free-kick was drilled into the Barcelona defensive wall.

Straight up the other end in this frantic start to the game, Rivaldo found himself with a shooting opportunity in the Leeds penalty area but ran into a white brick wall of six Leeds players.

The opening exchanges felt more like a basketball game than a football one with both teams desperate to attack the opposition goal at the earliest opportunity after every turnover of possession. Viduka won a free-kick from Fernandez Abelardo on the wide left almost near the corner flag. The free-kick looked best placed for a cross into the box and Lee Bowyer's effort into the back post was perhaps intended for Viduka or Erik Bakke waiting there. Instead, the ball evaded everyone including the desperate grasp of goalkeeper Richard Dutruel and incredibly found the back of the net. Pandemonium. If the score was to finish this way, it would be mission accomplished for Leeds but there would still be over 90 minutes to play, and the breathless tempo of the game only suggested more goals were coming. Leeds will have been aware that the Catalans overturned a three-goal deficit in the previous season to eliminate Chelsea in the knockout stages of the competition.

Barcelona looked to reply instantly from the kick-off and won a free-kick in a very handsome position 25 yards out and central to Paul Robinson's goal after Luis Enrique's charge forward was thwarted by a trailing leg of Bakke. Rivaldo won the argument with Xavi over who would take it, but his effort was scuffed harmlessly wide much to the delight of the Kop end behind the goal who cheekily taunted the Brazillian superstar with a chorus of "Who the f**king hell are you?".

Alan Smith's tenacity was causing the Barcelona back three problems just as it was Paulo Maldini and co in AC Milan's visit earlier in the group. The Rothwell-born striker was playing as the pumped-up representative of the fans in the stands and came close to doubling United's advantage as his low effort from a Bowyer cutback was parried around the post by Dutruel for a corner.

Midway through the first half Oliver Dacourt received his obligatory booking for a foul on Luis Enrique and escaped further punishment whilst on this tightrope– unlike his fate in the qualifying round at home to 1860 Munich - after other illegal interventions on Xavi and Simao.

Robinson was called upon for the first, but certainly not the last time on the night on 23 minutes when his quick reactions were needed to deny a glancing Rivaldo header from a wide free-kick with a left-handed save pushing the ball away to the relative safety of a corner. It was at this stage of the game that Barcelona had started to gain some dominance in possession and were looking the more dangerous after Leeds's energetic and combative start.

The Elland Road crowd was on top form for this one, knowing that they needed to be the twelve-man against their most illustrious opponents. Every Leeds tackle and Barcelona mishap was cheered, and white shirts were roared on whenever they charged up the pitch.

With eight minutes to go in the first half, Leeds thrice threatened the Barcelona goal. Firstly, a speculative effort from Dacourt flew well over the crossbar before some neat link-up between Smith, Bowyer and Viduka resulted in Bowyer being denied by Dutruel from seven yards out. From a resultant throw-in, Gary Kelly's teasing cross was met by the diving head of Viduka which went just wide.

Leeds finished the half very strong and won numerous corners and free-kicks in goal-challenging positions. However, Barcelona had the final chance in the one minute of added time to equalise, but Robinson was again equal to Rivaldo's low-driven free-kick from 23 yards. The Leeds players returned down the tunnel for half-time to a deafening roar of approval from the Elland Road stands.

Early in the second half, Smith proceeded to charge at Abelardo who had struggled to mark the Leeds youngster all game who cynically stopped him at source with a professional foul. Technically Abelardo was the last man back but was spared a dismissal and settled for a yellow card due to the large distance between the incident and the goal. Viduka was also causing problems for the Barcelona defence when driving forwards and his hold-up play was key in allowing his teammates to rise up the pitch as Leeds strived to resist the temptation of sitting back and defending their lead. Despite a positive start, this began to prove difficult as the visitors asserted themselves as the game approached its final half-hour. Robinson pulled off the save of the night on 55 minutes with a superb reflex save with his fingertips to deny a certain goal-bound header from Alfonso. Commentator on the evening for ITV Peter Drury admitted afterwards that he was calling 'goal'. The game had a fascinating sub-plot with the battle between the best striker in the world Rivaldo and the rookie goalkeeper Robinson. The latter again came out on top with an almost replica save of a free-kick to the one that occurred in first-half stoppage time - this time Robinson saving to his right-hand side. Dacourt, on the other hand, seemed as though he was desperate for an early bath and scythed down Rivaldo as he ran at goal but yet again escaped further punishment by a very lenient Norwegian referee in Terje Hauge. The resultant Rivaldo free-kick again resulted in Robinson saving low to his right-hand post. David O'Leary eventually chose to no longer take a risk on Dacourt and replaced him with Australian Jacob Burns, who was brought was as someone who could initially strengthen the reserves and who had only made his first start for the club a week prior in the home win against Charlton Athletic. Danny Mills was walking a different kind of tightrope to Dacourt in that if he was to be booked in this game, he would miss Group H's conclusion at the San Siro a fortnight later due to picking up two bookings previously in the competition. Mills narrowly avoided a booking after a late lunge on Dani García as Leeds were beginning to feel the pressure of men in red and blue stripes knocking relentlessly at the door.

With twenty minutes remaining Rivaldo had finally beaten his young nemesis in the Leeds goal. Five Leeds defenders had surrounded Alfonso but he managed to lay a pass off to Rivaldo who was making a late run towards the penalty area whose instinctive shot took a deflection and bobbled past Robinson into the bottom right corner. The goal though, to the delight of the Leeds crowd, was instantly disallowed as Simao in an offside position was deemed to be having an active interference in play.

As the game reached its final stages the West Yorkshire rain began to hammer down just as it did so relentlessly in the AC Milan game weeks earlier. "We're Leeds and were proud of it" screamed the home fans and proud they could be as their team defended resolutely as the visitors dominated with 61% possession in the second half. Leeds United, humbled, and humiliated by Barcelona in the Camp Nou forty-two days earlier were now just minutes away from incredibly booking their place in the second group phase in front of their own fans and with a game to spare, whilst in turn eliminating the Catalan superstars. The minutes and seconds though for anyone of Leeds persuasion were ticking agonisingly slowly as the fourth official indicated there would be four added minutes amid 34,485 deafening whistles. Leeds looked to have come through unscathed, until painfully, in the last of those four added minutes, Gerard was denied by a post from six yards and the ball rebounded kindly into the path of no other than Rivaldo who turned the ball goal bound. Elland Road in an instant went from fever pitch to deafly silent but for the relieved celebrations of the Barcelona players and bench whose very involvement in the Champions League was rescued by the goal and the point it earned. Referee Hauge blew almost instantly after the restart as tempers of this keenly contested tie had boiled over with a melee between both sets of players with Puyol and Smith at the centre of the drama before both teams were separated. Elsewhere Lee Bowyer was on his knees, O'Leary's face was a picture of deflation, and man of the match Paul Robinson was consoled by goalkeeping coach Steve Sutton

Speaking a week later in his programme notes O'Leary stated "I'm philosophical about most things in life and I've been around football long enough to know these things happen, but I have to say it took me several days to get over that one. I was reliving it, going through all the ifs and buts, and wondering just how the ball managed to fall to Rivaldo of all people when it came back off the post".

Dominic Matteo also revealed that no one said a word in the dressing room post-match due to feeling so deflated and it took a few days for the players to get over.

Robinson was rightly pleased with his outstanding performance and showdown with the holder of the Ballon d'Or. "You know you are doing well when you see a player like Rivaldo tearing his hair out in frustration. That is a memory that will stay with me forever but so will the terrible feeling I had when he finally beat me", quoted the young goalkeeper. His manager later reflected on his deputy goalkeeper's sterling display in *Leeds United on Trial*. "Robbo truly proved his exceptional talent that night. If he can do it against the likes of Rivaldo in the Champions League, he can do it anywhere".

Despite the overwhelming sense of frustration in the United dressing room, a point against Barcelona was useful in that it kept their opponents at arm's reach away and meant that Leeds's fate was still in their own hands going into the final fixture of Group H. The point also guaranteed a UEFA Cup space for continued European involvement that season as the lowest they could finish in the group was third. However, it would have been a very different ending to the evening had the final whistle been blown 30 seconds earlier. The goal was recorded by UEFA at four minutes thirty-seven seconds and O'Leary later told how referee Hauge ate at a restaurant owned by his friend in Leeds City Centre that evening. The restaurateur threw his watch on the table in protest of the added time when delivering his meal to Hague such was his frustration. Now, from being seconds away from heroism, qualification, and recording one of the most impressive results in the club's history, Leeds knew they had the arduous task of getting a result against AC Milan in the San Siro two weeks later whilst Barcelona had the somewhat easier task of needing to beat a fading Besiktas team in Spain.

Dom Matteo Scored a Really Good Goal in the San Siro

AC Milan (Away)

UEFA Champions League, 1st Group Phase, Matchday 6

The first nine days of November 2000 have gone down as some of the most memorable In Leeds United's history. A visit from Liverpool in the Premier League and a do-or-die clash at Milan's San Siro to conclude Group H were vital to United's season even in these relatively embryonic stages of the season. The results and events of the two games are still revered and sung about to this day.

However, the form in which they entered the games was far from ideal. Had Leeds held on for thirty seconds longer against Barcelona they would perhaps have been able to approach a tricky run of fixtures in a less pressurised way. From welcoming European royalty in Barcelona, Leeds's next assignment was a banana skin of a local derby with Bradford City. Valley Parade was the venue, situated just 14 miles away from Elland Road. Despite the proximity, the lack of previous fixtures between the two sides and their differing fortunes hardly contributed to a fierce rivalry but there were West Yorkshire bragging rights available in a Sunday afternoon clash. An acrobatic effort from City debutant Stan Collymore put 'The Bantams' ahead midway through the first half before Mark Viduka headed home a Dominic Matteo cross with ten minutes left on the clock to spare United's blushes.

Attention quickly turned to domestic cup action as The Whites travelled to First Division side Tranmere Rovers in the third round of the League Cup. The League Cup represented the most realistic chance for O'Leary's young side to gain their first piece of silverware but after a gruelling derby-day draw only two days previously there were changes made to the line-up with fringe players Danny Hay, Jacob Burns, Matthew Jones, and Darren Huckerby all making rare starts. The latter looked to have secured a passage into the fourth round with minimal fuss when he scored a first-half brace. The second half proved anything but routine, however. Goals from Andy Parkinson and Wayne Alison sent the tie into extra time – the last thing O'Leary needed in this vital period – and just as the game was approaching a penalty shoot-out a late Parkinson winner sent the underdogs from Merseyside into the hat for the next round. United's manager labelled his team's second-half performance as a disgrace but lamented the fact that his team was forced into playing two games in three days and that England is the only country in world football that places these types of constraints on its teams' schedules. The type of argument we still hear from the likes of Pep Guardiola and Jurgen Klopp to this day.

Leeds then welcomed Tranmere's more illustrious city neighbours Liverpool FC to Elland Road in what turned out to be a Premier League classic. It was important for Leeds – sitting in tenth place - to gain some ground on The Reds who were occupying that all-important third Champions League place, six points ahead of The Whites. Leeds's defence was caught still sleeping at the beginning of this 11.30 am kick-off for the SKY Sports cameras and found themselves two goals behind within 18 minutes. This afternoon will always be remembered though for the exploits of Mark Viduka and his four goals that saw Leeds come from twice behind to snatch an important victory. His first came midway through the first half after Alan Smith had hassled Christian Ziege into a mistake and he equalised two minutes into the second half heading a Gary Kelly cross into the top corner. A goal from Vladimir Smicer put Liverpool back ahead on 61 minutes but the inspired Viduka was not to be outshone, grabbing his hat-trick equalising on 73 minutes and chipping over goalkeeper Sander Westerveld two minutes later to put Leeds in front for the first time in the match. Leeds held on to seal the three points and Viduka was mobbed by teammates, greeting his mother into the camera lens following him before his manager ran onto the pitch with outstretched arms to embrace him for his unprecedented performance. The striker had now well and truly answered those who criticised his early season hiatus at the Olympics following his big-money move from Celtic. He had now scored eleven goals in his last fourteen appearances since his maiden goal at home to Besiktas. "Playing in the Olympics really helped me because I now feel much stronger", was the justification given by the Aussie for his earlier representation for the 'Socceroos'. He had also gained an admirer from Leeds United's past in Allan Clarke who is immortalised in the club's history as one of their greatest-ever strikers and was the match-winning goal scorer in United's only ever FA Cup final win in 1972. Clarke praised the new number 9 by comparing him to a former player who had 9 on his back – Clarke's formidable strike partner Mick Jones who scored 77 goals in 220 appearances for Leeds United.

After a tricky spell for Leeds who had struggled for momentum in their Premier League campaign, not helped by a relentless injury list, the victory over Liverpool was the perfect tonic as preparations turned to a showdown with Italian giants AC Milan in the San Siro. If the Barcelona home game was Leeds United's biggest home game since their semi-final clash with the Catalans in 1975, the Milan trip was arguably the club's most important game since the subsequent final a quarter of a century earlier.

The showdown in the 'Group of Death' was tantalising enough as it was but attentions were drawn even further to the clash in the days leading to the encounter. Just as in 1973, a game involving Leeds United and AC Milan was played against a backdrop of accusations of bribery and match-fixing. Milan was already guaranteed a place in the next round. Barcelona needed to win at home to Besiktas to have any chance of progression whilst a point for Leeds in Milan would guarantee they would join the Italians in the second group stage. Should Leeds lose and Barcelona win, the two teams would be tied on eight points, but the Spanish team would advance due to their better head-to-head record in the games involving the two. The Spanish media claimed that a deal had been completed between Milan and Leeds that would ensure Milan would allow Leeds the draw needed to put themselves through alongside Milan and eliminate Barcelona in the process. However, Barcelona was reputed to have offered AC Milan a sum of €1.5 million to defeat Leeds. The sum worked out at €55,000 per member of Milan's 26-man squad to ensure their full attention and energies were put into this game which was essentially a dead rubber for the Italian outfit who were only playing for top spot in Group H. The story was further ignited when Spanish newspaper outlet *Catalan Sport* quoted Milan forward Jose Mari saying that he didn't believe being offered financial incentives to be illegal. When questioned on this his response was "If Joan Gaspart (Barcelona president) wants to give us something we will accept it in good faith". The rumours ended up being exactly that and the story was quashed when Milan's vice-president, Adriano Galliani, stated that "no director of Barcelona has made a proposition to AC Milan, its directors or its squad, of a win bonus". Milan manager Alberto Zaccherini was in no such charitable mood towards any other team anyway and convinced O'Leary that if his team was getting anything from his side on the night then they would have to earn it. Leeds Assistant Manager Eddie Gray was part of the Leeds squad (although was injured for the game) when allegations of the 1973 European Cup-Winners' Cup final were fixed in favour of Milan. When questioned for his opinions as United flew out to Italy the Scotsman rubbished the accusations as just 'newspaper talk'. Speaking even just before the rumours were running the mill, Jimmy Armfield – manager when Leeds reached the final of the competition 25 years previously – made the case of the continentals not having the same mindset when it came to fair competition and questioned Milan's motivations. "A lot will depend on Milan's attitude to the game. European players don't think like we think. They might be happier to see Leeds through than Barcelona. One thing I'm sure of, they won't want to lose in front of their own crowd. That's the problem Leeds have but I still think they can do it", he said.

Off the pitch, just six months after the murders of Christopher Loftus and Kevin Speight in Istanbul, a Leeds United fan was the victim of a stabbing assault on the eve of a game in Europe. *Calendar News* reported that A 31-year-old man suffered thirteen stab wounds in his groin, face, and left hand including a serious injury to his abdomen on the eve of the match after being attacked by pieces of a broken bottle in central Milan in the early hours of the morning. He was amongst a group of friends about to enter a disco when he was set upon by a group of Italian men. The group of Leeds supporters was reported to have run away after realising the Italian group they had encountered wasn't friendly but unfortunately one man slipped and was subsequently attacked and needed two emergency operations on the day of the match. His condition at the time was reported to be serious but not life-threatening.

Peter Ridsdale was praised for his cooperation during the previous tragic scenes in Istanbul earlier that year and reacted to the news to *Calendar News*. "It's appalling, and this year you look back at some of the things that have happened to the football club, time and time again, and just as we try and concentrate on what happens on the field, incidents like this one take place and it's devastating. I'm just delighted that on this occasion the young man is not critically injured and will hopefully make a full recovery", the United Chairman stated. West Yorkshire Police in Milan were keen to stress that the attack was completely unprovoked and not a result of hooliganism. Ridsdale decided to shield the Leeds United players from the news - in this pre-social media age - so soon after many of the team had gone through a similar ordeal. "So far we have tried to shield the team from the news; clearly when you travel you do not want to hear of incidents such as this". Ridsdale admitted that the news of the incident brought back memories of April's tragic events in Istanbul. 'I'm feeling pretty drained by the situation, to be frank,' he continued. 'Incidents like today bring the difficult times flooding back again", He said. 6,000 Leeds fans travelled to Italy, and they were bused from the airport into Milan where the Italian police imposed a total alcohol ban in bars and restaurants in response to the incident.

***

No expense was spared to make the Leeds team feel comfortable who stayed at nearby Lake Como in a beautiful villa called Vila d'Este and were flown out on a private jet that usually ferried around rock band U2. The team trained at the San Siro on the eve of the game and because of a mix-up with transportation from the team hotel, Peter Ridsdale was left behind. This brought a new superstition for the team at the expense of the United chairman after the game's outcome as he was no longer allowed to visit pre-match training sessions.

Aboard U2's jet were defensive trio Jonathan Woodgate, Danny Mills, and Lucas Radebe but there were concerns over each of their fitness. On the other hand, despite their strong Champions League form (Elland Road excepted) Milan's domestic form had struggled for momentum and they hadn't won since their Serie A campaign belatedly began on October 1st; winless in their last four league matches, leaving them languishing in mid-table. For those not a part of the 6,000-strong travelling army, the game was available live on Yorkshire Television with Manchester United again hogging the terrestrial limelight on ITV for their must-win clash with Dynamo Kyiv at Old Trafford. But this was a big night for English football. Despite United's aforementioned Cross-Pennines rivals winning the competition in 1998-99, success for English teams in the Champions League since it was rebranded was scarce. Arsenal had already booked their place in the second group stage, but it had taken them three attempts to do so. Leeds was on the cusp of clearing the first hurdle at their first attempt and from a group some experts predicted would be impossible for them to do so. Perhaps concerned that the chance of progression had passed his team by with the late concession to Barcelona at Elland Road, the Leeds manager spoke more in hope than expectations in his pre-match comments. "Given all the problems we had; it is a great tribute to the players that we know we can still reach the second group stage if we can get a draw in Milan. Our fate is still in our own hands". Milan will be my 22nd European game since I became manager and that's been a wonderful learning experience for me as a young manager. During those two years, we have faced a lot of adversity in one way or another, but we have come through together stronger and in good spirits. We are all looking forward to our night in the San Siro and in the end, you have to say what will be will be, and just hope we get our rewards in Milan", O'Leary said when interviewed at Vila d'Este.

Leeds enjoyed a light-hearted session in an eerie empty San Siro on the eve of the match and staged an 'Oldies vs Young'uns' 8 a side match. Such was the youthful nature of this squad, Paul Robinson (21) and Danny Mills (23) played for the 'Oldies' in a 3-2 victory for the seniors. The San Siro is of course shared between AC Milan and city rivals Internazionale. A recent signing for 'Inter' was Irishman Robbie Keane who signed from Coventry City in the summer of 2000 for £13 million. Living opposite the stadium in a luxury apartment block with club teammate – Brazilian superstar Ronaldo as a neighbour – Keane took the opportunity to pop by and say hello to his Irish national teammates Gary Kelly and Ian Harte.

On the victorious 'Oldies' team was Dominic Matteo - of Italian heritage - and who was enjoying a fine start to his Leeds career since his summer move from Liverpool. Speaking retrospectively in his autobiography *In My Defence* he mentioned how he went into the game in a very optimistic headspace. "Once the day of the game arrived in Milan, I felt good. I had a feeling the night was going to go well. I can't explain why, I just did. It might have been because I knew all of my Dad's family in Italy would be watching due to the game being shown live on television in their own country. Whatever the reason, I just felt confident from the moment I woke up that morning".

Leeds lined up alongside Milan completing the pre-game formalities of exchanging handshakes – the gesture of fair play which was hopefully going to be fulfilled in particularly by the Milan Players. No Leeds team had ever won in Italy before, and this was the tenth time an English team had taken to the San Siro pitch to face AC Milan in European competition, and not on any of these occasions did the English side leave it victorious. To further dispel any doubts that Milan was going to take the game easy, Zaccherini named a full-strength team of eleven internationals. That was more than could be said for Leeds. O'Leary was only able to name four out of a possible five substitutes in the

Liverpool game and on this night, he could only make six out of seven. Goalkeeper Danny Milosevic, Matthew Jones, Danny Hay, Jacob Burns, Alan Maybury, and Gareth Evans made up that bench - none of which could be described as first-team regulars with only a handful of appearances between them.

The referee who had the unenviable task of officiating this match under the microscope was no stranger to controversy. Kim Milton Nielsen was known to English football supporters as the man who had sent off David Beckham for his innocuous yet petulant kick out at Diego Simeone in England's World Cup defeat to Argentina two summers previously. Another talking point before the game which was to play effect on proceedings was the state of the San Siro pitch which had long been renowned for not matching the standards of its surroundings due to the lack of sunlight it attracts from being blocked by the towering stands, and on this occasion, it was not helped by incessant rain in Milan. The stadium was selected to host the final in May 2001 and the centre of the pitch from goal to goal was scheduled to be re-laid after the conclusion of this match.

From the kick-off, there was a fast tempo start to the game but lacked cutting edge which wasn't helped by the playing surface. Milan made an aggressive start looking to attack each time they overturned possession in jest of their Italian defensive 'catenaccio' style of play. The first clear chance came after ten minutes. Brazilian left-winger Serginho turned and raced away from Gary Kelly on the wide left just inside United's half. In this first episode of a fascinating duel between the two players on that side of the pitch, Kelly tried to keep pace with Serginho but slipped as he did so. Lee Bowyer made a run to cover the Irishman but once he was beaten Kelly decided enough was enough and brought the Brazilian down via his trailing right arm for a free-kick just outside the penalty area. Demitri Albertini's subsequent free-kick was whipped invitingly across the face of the goal but evaded a touch from Ukrainian striker Andriy Shevchenko at the back post.

The experienced Milan skipper Paulo Maldini took his first opportunity on thirteen minutes to make a lunge on his irritant opponent from the Elland Road tie in Alan Smith and marked his card. Meanwhile, as Leeds gained their first corner of the match news came through that Barcelona had taken the lead at home to Besiktas and if that score was to maintain, Leeds had to ensure they came out of the San Siro unscathed. As the game settled with both teams sussing each other out like the first round of a heavyweight boxing match - Leeds had their fair share of corners and set-pieces close to Dida's goal but could not make any meaningful threats from them. Curiously in retrospect, at the heart of Milan's defence was future Brazilian World Cup winner Roque Junior. The central defender went on to have an ill-fated and highly underwhelming loan spell in Leeds's Premier League relegation season three years later and was having an uneasy night dealing with the attack of Smith, Viduka, and Lee Bowyer.

Milan had a decent chance at taking the lead midway through the first half when Leonardo played a ball into Shevchenko who made a run into the penalty area, but he was forced into a wider shooting angle by Radebe who got a foot to the Ukrainian's shot which deflected over for a corner. A few minutes later a nonchalant header back from Ian Harte intended for his goalkeeper Paul Robinson was intercepted in a flash from the quick-witted Oliver Bierhoff but thankfully for Leeds, it flashed wide of the goal.

It became clearer that Leeds would need a positive result on the night as Barcelona doubled their lead elsewhere in Group H and Leeds was beginning to retreat as Milan pressed forward. Potential disaster loomed midway through the first half after Serginho played a one-two in the box with Bierhoff and referee Nielsen spotted Kelly blocking Serginho's effort at a cross with his raised elbow and pointed to the penalty spot. Shevchenko - who had already had seven European goals to his name that campaign - took a long run up for his penalty to the noise of 6,000 Yorkshire whistles designed to deter him behind Robinson's goal. The Leeds goalkeeper dived to his left as the ball travelled to his right, but Shevchenko's effort hit a post and rolled harmlessly out for a goal kick as the Leeds fan's whistles turned to ecstatic and relieved cheers. Soon after, both teams saw promising-looking free-kicks from Albertini and Harte respectively reach their target but comfortably claimed by each goalkeeper.

As the clock approached half-time some lackadaisical defending from Radebe allowed Leonardo to create an almost carbon copy of the chance he made for Shevchenko earlier in the game. The result was also the same as Shevchenko's shot, this time from a more favourable angle was expertly intercepted and deflected out for a corner by Radebe as he atoned for his earlier error. From the resultant corner, Bierhoff was allowed a free header which went narrowly unpunished, and shortly after Robinson was at hand to deny Serginho's low-driven effort as Leeds fans were counting down the seconds on the large scoreboard situated to their right-hand side for half-time.

In the final minute of the half, Mark Viduka – industrious yet quiet in front of goal compared to his exploits four days earlier – forced a corner. What came next was a moment still sung by Leeds United supporters to this day. Bowyer's out-swinging corner was met by Dominic Matteo who rose highest at the corner of the six-yard box, and he directed his header into the near post. The header beat Dida who got a hand to the ball, but he could only turn it into the inside of the side netting. The goal was prophetic of Matteo's morning optimism of playing in his ancestors' homeland. The goal may have been against the run of play, but it meant as the two teams retreated into the dressing rooms for the interval that Milan would now have to score twice to prevent Leeds from progressing to the last 16.

That was still to be no easy feat. AC Milan had scored in 23 consecutive European home games and made their intentions to get back into the game immediately clear with Shevchenko blasting a shot from the edge of the area over the bar just seconds after the restart and minutes later Robinson was forced into a save from a half volley from Leonardo. The introduction of Croatian midfielder Zvonimir Boban early on in the second half gave Milan a different attacking dimension. As the game approached the hour mark Serginho placed a tempting low cross into the corridor of uncertainty between the goal and the defenders facing it. Radebe outstretched his right leg to get a touch which looped over Robinson. It was a heart-in-mouth situation as the ball looked for a split second to be turned in for an own goal, but it was instead a timely intervention from the South African skipper to deny Milan.

Leeds would have felt a sense of déjà vu to this game similar to their last European game at home to Barcelona. A goal ahead from the first half against the odds with their more fancied opponents now asserting themselves. Leeds needed all hands-on deck defensively as the minutes ticked by slowly, but David O'Leary felt averse to turning to his inexperienced bench and the patchworked eleven that started the game would go on to complete it.

Shevchenko seemingly desperate to atone for his earlier penalty miss came the closest yet from his catalogue of chances on 64 minutes. His head connected powerfully with a Boban cross and forced Robinson into a fingertip save over the crossbar.

With a quarter of the game remaining the moment which had felt inevitable came as Milan grabbed an equaliser. The pace and directness of Serginho had been causing Kelly problems all evening but as Serginho entered the area Kelly could curse the atrocious pitch for him missing his tackle which bobbled up and down on the surface and allowed the Brazilian winger to get away a shot and convert past the onrushing Robinson into the far corner of the goal. From being in top position in the live standings of Group H Leeds were now just one more concession away from elimination.

The goal had raised the noise level from Milan's support which was far from capacity with large pockets of empty seats visible across the stadium in a 52,289 crowd. There were initially clear nerves from the Leeds players in the minutes following the equaliser but as the game entered the final ten minutes they had started to settle as they could see the finish line and were helped by Milan losing the same intensity that got them back into the game. Two added minutes were indicated but there was to be no repeat of the late dagger through the heart which Rivaldo had delivered a fortnight earlier as Kim Milton Nielsen put his whistle to his mouth after a boot forward from Maldini. White shirts almost in tandem stood arms aloft in triumph. The Italian Job was completed. No one had given Leeds United a chance when they were drawn alongside AC Milan and Barcelona alongside a nightmare scenario of a return to Istanbul back in August's draw. They were then given even less of a prayer when they were so brutally put in their place on opening night at Camp Nou.

Yet Leeds had qualified with nine points in second place of Group H and had eliminated Barcelona in the process.

Once the players were showered and changed, they were sent back out onto the pitch to salute 6000 delirious fans who had been kept behind for security reasons and give the usual wave and show off appreciation. A chant of "Leeds team give us a song" came from the away end to which each player duly obliged taking turns to start a chant from the Leeds United terrace songbook. Gary Kelly (who had just made his 300th appearance for the club) and renowned jokester was the one who volunteered first. As he approached the travelling hoards a loud cheer echoed before Kelly gestured for silence. After a short pause, the right-back jumped up and down on the spot shouting "Let's go f***ing metal" and had 6000 people doing the same in an instant. Kelly continued his stage act by again asking for silence before sitting down on the damp San Siro turf and singing, "Sit down if you hate Man U". "It was just a spur-of-the-moment thing, to be honest. Everyone was enjoying the evening and when the fans started singing, some of the boys just said, 'Go for it'. We were enjoying ourselves and the fans and the rest of the boys joined in. I don't think anyone who was there will ever forget such a lovely evening" Kelly said.

By this time the rest of the team wanted in on this wonderful yet rare embrace between players and supporters. Alan Smith sang the appropriate lyrics of "We're Leeds and we're proud of it" and even chairman Peter Ridsdale joined in the festivities playing it safe with the chorus of the club's anthem 'Marching on Together'. Lee Bowyer – so often the star of the show on the pitch during this campaign – demonstrated that his talents didn't extend to singing. His effort at singing an indecipherable chant brought a return from the stands of "What the f***king hell was that" and a playful chasing on the pitch from his teammates. It was a moment neither supporters nor players wanted to end, and it took the on-duty stadium police to encourage the Leeds team to eventually vacate the pitch. BBC Radio 5 Live broadcaster Alan Green described the scenes as "the most powerful bonding between fans and players" he had ever witnessed. There was a party back at their Lake Como hotel later that night. The team was scheduled to fly back home in readiness for their game away to Chelsea at Stamford Bridge four days later. But as a reward for their incredible feat, Ridsdale had paid for the team to stay one more night at their hotel which had so impressed even these wealthy Premier League stars although many would not see their beds until the early hours of the next morning.

The match-fixing side story wouldn't go away after the match with Barcelona incensed that Leeds was able to get the result they required against Milan and made calls for a UEFA inquiry, but nothing came of the matter. A buoyant O'Leary rightfully praised his team's efforts and additionally did not waste the chance to twist the knife on Barcelona: "A few people gave us some stick after we lost heavily in Barcelona. This is our answer. I tend to remember these things and as for Frank De Boer, I would be interested to know what he thinks about tonight. He was very quick to have a go at Alan Smith who happened to have a great game against Milan tonight. I would have settled for a 1-1 scoreline before the game but looking back on the match I thought we played well and deserved to win. To have got through at the first attempt and from the most difficult group is a quite remarkable achievement for us and one of which we can all feel very proud. It just shows how far we have come in a couple of years. I'm thrilled for everyone at the club and for all those fans who have backed us all the way".

Looking back two decades later O'Leary pointed out how Milan manager Albert Zaccheroni had invited him and his coaching staff for a post-match beer. "I think they were pleased we had got through and Barcelona hadn't. They probably felt Barcelona were contenders and we weren't" O'Leary told *The Athletic*. Zaccheroni certainly spoke complimentary of his opponents that evening post-match. "Leeds have demonstrated what a good team they are. They can go as far as any other team left in the competition after their results in this very tough group. It is not about a team's history in the Champions League, it is about how they are playing now, and Leeds have had some very good results indeed. We played to win the game, Milan always does their best, and it is unfortunate for Barcelona that they are out, but only two teams can go through" said the Milan boss.

So, from escaping one of the hardest possible draws in qualifying to navigate their way through a ridiculously challenging group in their maiden Champions League season, Leeds United fans could look forward with anticipation to the second group stage draw. When asked for his opinions on the draw O'Leary commented "Knowing us we will probably have Real Madrid and Lazio and I'll say, 'Well it'll be a miracle getting out of this group' but we'll try!".

The Galacticos Come to Town

Real Madrid (Home)

UEFA Champions League 2nd Group Phase, Matchday 1

Whilst no team was enjoying the Champions League more than Leeds United, their continued involvement was not in the best interest of their stuttering Premier League campaign. Leeds had lost in the league after both returns from Europe previously and after Milan, they travelled to Stamford Bridge to face a Chelsea side who were also having a slow start to the season. Mark Viduka continued his rich vein of goalscoring form to put Leeds ahead but a Gus Poyet goal for the hosts meant the spoils were shared. The point won was a satisfactory one as far as Leeds were concerned and chairman Peter Ridsdale was still overcome with pride from the club progressing to the second round of the Champions League and saw it fit to publicly heap praise on the team and his manager. "This is normally the time when I thank you (the supporters) for your support, and of course I do again, but for once I would like to finish by thanking David and the team for a magnificent few weeks. Thank You", he wrote to conclude his programme notes before the home clash with West Ham United a week later.

That fixture with 'The Hammers' left home supporters leaving Elland Road disappointed in the league again. A rare goal from defender Nigel Winterburn on the stroke of half-time gave West Ham all three points in West Yorkshire leaving Leeds marooned in mid-table. It was another defender that caught the eye in that encounter though. 22-year-old Rio Ferdinand impressed on-watchers with his commanding performance, shutting out Viduka and Alan Smith. Ferdinand already had long-term admirers in Leeds United who had attempted to sign the centre-back in the summer but with their stock high with European progression and their defensive resources repeatedly depleted with injury, Leeds saw enough on the day to step up their efforts in signing the defender.

A fee of £18 million was suggested which was eye-watering at the time and made front-page headlines as well as the back. It would be a British record fee and the most anyone in world football had forked out for a defender. He may have had nine England caps to his name and made Glen Hoddle's 1998 World Cup squad as a 19-year-old, but he was hardly a regular pick for the Three Lions, and eyebrows were raised at the price tag of such a young player. Elsewhere, the recent impressive performances of Paul Robinson and Alan Smith did not go unnoticed as caretaker manager Peter Taylor selected the pair for the upcoming England international away to Italy. However, his club boss saw this as an unnecessary hindrance for Smith and negotiated a recall before he could board the plane to Turin. Explaining his decision as preventing the youngster from burning out with such a heavy fixture schedule O'Leary told Don Warters, "He has played week in and week out and seems very tired. I don't think it will be too much of a blow for Alan because he's only 19 and there will be plenty more internationals to come. He has many years ahead of him". A tired performance from Smith against West Ham ratified his manager's decision whilst Robinson did travel but was an unused substitute in England's 1-0 defeat to the 'Azzurri'.

***

Unlike today's Champions League format where teams that qualify for the Last 16 of the competition initial go on to play two-legged knockout ties to decide who will progress to the quarter-finals - from the 1999-00 through to the 2002-

03 editions, the remaining sixteen teams entered a second group stage, again with the top two teams qualifying. This guaranteed another six guaranteed money-spinning ties to the competing clubs but wreaked havoc with domestic schedules and with Leeds struggling on the domestic front this format threatened to be counterproductive to their threadbare squad's league ambitions. The draw for the second group stage was made swiftly after the conclusion of the first round and there was little planning time as the next round of Champions League games were scheduled for just a fortnight later.

Seeding was determined by the UEFA coefficients and the participants' first group stage positions. The four best-ranked group winners were seeded in Pot 1 and the remaining four in Pot 2. Group runners-up were seeded to Pots 3 and 4 accordingly. If there were any regrets left in the San Siro from Leeds it would have been their failure to see out the match with their 0-1 lead intact which would have seen them emerge from Group H as group winners and with it guarantee them a seeding position in pots one or two. Instead, they were placed in pot 4 so the chances of another tough group to negotiate was likely. Joining them in pot 4 were French team Lyon, Greeks Panathinaikos and thankfully Galatasaray so again Leeds avoided the possibility of another logistical nightmare of the two teams being paired together. It was the first ever time that three teams from England had made it to the last 16, however, teams from the same country or the same first-round group could not be drawn together at this stage removing any chance of an all-English battle with Arsenal or Manchester United or another tie with AC Milan.

David O'Leary was speaking with irony and humour of Leeds United's luck when he predicted Leeds would be paired with Real Madrid and Lazio and with it another ludicrously tough 'Group of Death'. But it was a prophesy that

Mystic Meg would have been proud of as Leeds were indeed paired with the European Champions and the Italian Champions. Joining them to complete the draw was Brussels-based side Anderlecht. Whilst on paper the Belgians seemed a less daunting task than Madrid and Lazio, Anderlecht were champions of the Belgian Pro League (they were currently on route to another title win where they would lose only once) and had a fine recent European record finishing top of their first-round group ahead of Manchester United and had won all three of their home fixtures. Elsewhere, Arsenal too had a challenging group consisting of Bayern Munich, Olympique Lyonnais, and Spartak Moscow whilst Manchester United had the more favourable task of facing Austrian's Sturm Graz, Panathinaikos, and the previous year's finalists Valencia. Group D unsurprisingly, involving the Whites looking like a small fish in a large shark-infested pond, was again dubbed the 'Group of Death' and if Leeds were to progress, they would have to do it the hard way again. Surely lightning couldn't strike twice.

Yet, Dominic Matteo recalls the squad's reaction was again one of elation in his autobiography *In My Defence*. "We were on the training pitch when the draw was made and one of the staff came out to tell us. Again, the lads thought he was pulling our legs. It wasn't that we wanted an easy draw after already having survived one 'Group of Death'. More than we thought we couldn't be that lucky again and get the chance to play against even more of the best teams in the best stadiums. Others may have expected us to be gutted by such a tough-looking group, but we were delighted. The feeling was, 'let's keep enjoying it'" he recalled. Other members of the squad were equally optimistic. Mark Viduka spoke before the Madrid game to the matchday programme stating "It is a big achievement to go through because there are so many huge clubs in the last 16. But I really think we won't stop there. We can go on from this group as well. It is the same as the last group when we were drawn with Barcelona and AC Milan. No one thought we would go through, but I think we can do it again". Viduka's strike partner Alan Smith was another who was excited rather than daunted by the prospect of another gruelling group. "The great thing is we have three more big nights at Elland Road starting with Real Madrid. It is important that we continue to take each game as it comes" he said.

The most intriguing of the teams Leeds was drawn with was obvious in Real Madrid. Fans from older generations or those who knew their history instantly saw a connection between the two clubs. In August 1962, Don Revie in his first managerial role at Leeds United made the bold decision to change the club's home strip colours from the blue and gold – traditional to the city of Leeds – to all white mimicking Real Madrid. The Spanish giants were an example to all in world football. They had won the first five editions of the European Cup with household names such as Alfredo Di Stefano and Ferenc Puskas. British attentions were drawn to them in 1960 when a crowd of 127,621 crowded into Hampden Park and hundreds of thousands more found a television set to see Madrid defeat Eintracht Frankfurt in the European Cup final in what is widely regarded as one of the greatest football matches ever played. Leeds, in 1962 were largely irrelevant compared to Madrid and recently only narrowly avoided relegation to the Third Division of English Football, and the city of Leeds were more renowned as a rugby league hotbed. Many ridiculed Revie's brash gesture of imitating the best team in the world, but he was adamant and stuck to his guns. "They're the best and that's what we want to be", he responded at the time. Leeds first wore their all-white strip in a pre-season friendly against Leicester City. Promotion back to the top flight was eventually won and his team became arguably the most revered and reviled team in equal measure over the following decade in the late 1960's and early 70's. Revie was obsessed with conquering Europe, inspired by that dominant Madrid team but the closest he would come would be the semi-finals in 1970 and the team he had built would make it one step further in 1975 a year after he left his post to become manager of the England national team. The remarkable period of success (alongside so many near misses) that Leeds enjoyed under Revie's stewardship led to the all-white strips being adopted proudly as part of the club's image to this day.

So, when fate placed Leeds United and Real Madrid together, it was a match-up that caught the imagination of many who were quick to point out that this would be the first time the two clubs had met. In a competitive sense, they were correct, but the two clubs were actually part of a four-team pre-season friendly tournament in La Linea in August 1981 which also included local side Sporting Gijon and Yugoslav outfit Partizan Belgrade. After beating Sporting 3-2 Leeds went on to face Real. Madrid had it stipulated in a contract that they must wear their famous *Blanco* (white) kit denying Leeds the chance to wear their adopted colours. They also couldn't wear their change all-yellow strips as television organisers advised they should borrow Sporting Gijon's black and white stripes to avoid a colour clash. A Leeds team which included their current assistant boss Eddie Gray lost 3-0 in a controversial match which saw United end the game with nine men after Derek Parlane and Arthur Graham were dismissed.

Real Madrid's participation in the competition, usually almost a permanent fixture, was a curious one in the 2000-01 season. Despite being the holders of the European Cup, they were only here defending their crown thanks to their 3-0 win against compatriots Valencia in the previous season's final as they had finished as low as fifth in La Liga in 1999-00. They were in the initial stages of President Florentino Perez's 'Galacticos' (meaning galaxy of stars) project which saw them collect the biggest stars in world football over the first few years of the noughties. The current crop included names such as Roberto Carlos, captain Fernando Hierro, Fernando Morinetes, Raul and Claude Makelele, and in later seasons would be joined by superstars such as Ronaldo, David Beckham, and Zinedine Zidane. Their shiny new toy in 2000 though came in the form of Portuguese midfielder Luis Figo. Madrid had finally secured the services of Figo from bitter rivals Barcelona after an aggressive approach in a protracted and highly documented transfer saga which received a world record transfer fee. Real's travel plans to Yorkshire were nearly disrupted when Leeds-Bradford Airport was closed to all other airborne transport due to inclement weather just as the team's plane was about to land but they escaped any inconvenience and were able to touch down to fog-bound Leeds without any hassle. Among the Madrid contingent was Englishman Steve McManaman formerly of Liverpool - and a close friend of Dominic Matteo. McManaman was enjoying a productive spell abroad even scoring in the previous year's final in Paris. Matteo was staying in the Oulton Hotel in Leeds city centre as temporary accommodation after his summer move. The hotel was the base of choice for most visiting teams to Elland Road and Real Madrid was no different, so Matteo went down to meet for a coffee and reunion with his old friend on the eve of the game. Not only did he see McManaman at the hotel bar but also all of the Madrid squad enjoying more than one alcoholic beverage with whom the Leeds defender mingled but restricting himself strictly to coffee. It wasn't just the current superstars present at The Oulton. The stars of Madrid's success in the 1950s and 60s and the now late yet immortal footballing legends of Alfredo Di Stefano and Ferenc Puskas were enjoying themselves in a quiet corner. The pair were flown to and treated like royalty wherever Real Madrid went. The relaxed nature of the Madrid players continued into matchday where they enjoyed a leisurely shopping trip in the afternoon and on reflection their body language compared to those of the Leeds players in the customary line up for the Champions League is noticeable of a set of teams that have been there, done that and got the winner's medals to show for it and a team where such occasions were still a novelty. Real Madrid, looking calm and composed, standing leaning back, Leeds shuffling on their feet, nervous expressions, and some using the occasion for last-minute stretches.

As if welcoming Real Madrid wasn't enough for Leeds United to deal with it was a case of Madrid today and tomorrow Rio as news emerged that a fee of £18 million was agreed to take Ferdinand from Upton Park to Elland Road and the defender was due to sign the day after the game. Peter Ridsdale justified his frivolous purchase to ITV before the Real Madrid clash. "We are spending 18 million pounds on a player that the manager believes is the missing piece of the jigsaw puzzle. Our income stream comes from being successful in Europe – through advertising, TV revenue, and sponsorship and that's going to be enhanced by players that will help keep us in Europe year on and year out and we believe that Rio will (do that)", he said. The fee shattered the former record of £13 million spent on a defensive player when Argentine Walter Samuel swapped Boca Juniors for AS Roma four months prior. Leeds was thinking long term however with Ferdinand's youth and potential and that was reflected with a five-and-a-half-year contract worth an estimated £30,000 a week (an increase of £8,000 on his weekly wage at Upton Park). The transfer also brought the net spend of David O'Leary's managerial reign to £42.35 spent against incoming transfer fees in just over two years in charge.

O'Leary was looking for a reaction from his troops following the West Ham defeat in which he described his team as having "no sparkle" in their performance. Pre-game the Leeds manager again bemoaned the depth of his squad hindering his team's progression at home and abroad. "We want to do well and get back into the UEFA Champions League next year through the Premier League, but I don't think it is possible to sustain a campaign on so many fronts with so few fit players in the squad", he mentioned in his programme notes. In his pre-match press conference, he stressed the importance of United's home games in advancing from Group D. "You have to avoid getting beat at home. You know in the Bernabéu or Lazio you won't get much. That is why it is important that we do well at home" he said.

The romance of the tie was not lost on the world's media. It was the first time that campaign that ITV had decided to overlook Manchester United and Arsenal when picking their solitary game for national terrestrial coverage. The game also attracted the largest interest in a match staged by UEFA in that season to date with coverage going out to over 200 countries from 23 separate television stations situated in Elland Road's ancient West Stand.

Leeds was entering the game in poor form in general despite their European progression with only one win in nine games and a glance at the team sheets indicated how tough a task it would be for Leeds to arrest that form on the night. If Leeds was about to have the most expensive British player, Real Madrid had the most expensive in the world, period, with Luis Figo.

Jonathan Woodgate who had barely trained since getting injured in the home victory over Liverpool nearly three weeks prior was patched up and placed into the starting line-up partnering Lucas Radebe in the centre of defence and a makeshift midfield line saw full-backs Gary Kelly and Dominic Matteo and on the right and left sides respectively. A second-half booking for Olivier Dacourt in the San Siro ruled the Frenchman out through suspension and Jacob Burns took his place in the heart of the midfield. As if to further display the gulf in depth between the teams and highlight United's unceasing injury woes, the away bench accommodated five Spain internationals whereas only two of the substitutes occupying the home dug-out had seen Premier League minutes so far that season.

Real (meaning Royal in Spanish after being granted Royal status by King Alfonso XIII in 1920) were again asserting themselves as the Royal family of European football winning two of the last three Champions League trophies after a 22-year hiatus from continental glory. They were led by future World Cup-winning manager Vicente Del Bosque, and like Leeds, were splashing the cash with six summer signings totalling a colossal for the time €75 million.

Radebe led his team in all-white forcing Real this time into their all-black number out into a raucous atmosphere where all but 200 of the 36,794 crowd were anticipating a famous home victory.

Madrid created the opening chance of the night after five minutes. A wide in-swinging free-kick from Figo into the six-yard box was only partially dealt with by Ian Harte and fell to the feet of the unmarked Guti but he blazed his effort over. Just a minute later Leeds almost drew first blood. Gary Kelly drew a late challenge from Roberto Carlos on the wide right. The free-kick allowed Leeds to get bodies forward and Lee Bowyer's kick was flown high into the Madrid penalty area. 19-year-old stopper Ikas Casillas (promoted from the youth team to win the competition at the end of the previous season) departed his goal line to collect the cross but missed it as the ball fell to the feet of Jonathan

Woodgate. Woodgate sorted his feet out to unleash a shot with the goal at his mercy but could only strike a post and the ball rebounded onto the head of Mark Viduka and then out for a goal-kick.

Figo never seemed far from the action throughout the game and was beginning to gain a reputation as a yellow card collector in Spain and missed Madrid's previous La Liga game through suspension. He was booked for simulation within the first ten minutes of the game after theatrically attempting to win a penalty from Woodgate. The Leeds defender gave the Portuguese something to go to ground about moments later, midway into the Leeds half, and he was also carded meaning the pair's duel would be played out on a tightrope for the majority of the match. The early bookings from Dutch referee Dick Jol prevented the same free-flowing intensity observers of the Leeds versus Barcelona game at Elland Road enjoyed and several innocuous fouls were pulled up upon meaning a very stop start feel to the match.

After the initial fast start with both teams going close the game settled midway through the first half and Madrid began to dominate as expected and enjoyed as much as 74 percent of the possession which started to uncharacteristically silence the Elland Road crowd. Figo was prevented from enjoying one of his more productive evenings in the first half and wasted a free-kick in a good position shooting harmlessly wide of Paul Robinson's goal. Steve McManaman – who had a habit of being on the winning side against Leeds - was playing the role of a pantomime villain and was playfully jeered on his every touch by the home crowd. The Liverpudlian's neat pass played in Raul Gonzales for his first effort of the night which required Robinson to dive low and turn the ball around his post. Raul later came close after a one-two with Guti in the Leeds penalty area resulting in his curling effort striking the outside of a post.

With Leeds now perhaps looking towards the sanctuary of half-time they instead almost went ahead. Viduka forced Ivan Campo into a poor clearance close to his own goal into the path of Bowyer who crossed towards the back post. There Dominic Matteo rose higher than Geremi and headed powerfully and downwards but was denied by Casillas. Another chance presented itself just before the break when experienced Spain and Madrid Captain Fernando Hierro brought down Viduka as he ran toward the goal. There was a chance for Harte to work his magic but after a long run-up, his low-driven effort was comfortably gathered by Casillas before the lurking Viduka could pounce on a rebound. The reflections on the half-time whistle would have been that Madrid were in control, but Leeds had created chances in the game so far but would need to try and assert themselves more in the second half.

On the teams' arrival for the second half the home crowd again seemed subdued, maybe in anticipation of the gulf in class that was to follow throughout the second period. Early on Raul aimed to chip the ball over Robinson, slightly out of position, but only found the roof of the net and he attempted the feat again shortly after, with the Leeds goalkeeper dealing with that attempt. A draw, needless to say, would represent a good result to open the group yet Leeds resisted the urge to protect a point and tried to press forward when they could, yet they failed to sustain any period of concerted pressure on the Real defence.

David O'Leary had limited options to make a difference from defence to turn the tide of the game and turned to winger Jason Wilcox to replace Jacob Burns on the hour mark. Wilcox was just returning from a knee operation and had only played fifteen minutes of action so far that season and was now being tasked with doubling that against the European champions highlighting again the plight of United's lengthy injury list. O'Leary would publicly reveal a few days later that he made the point to his assistant Eddie Gray that Leeds had a £100,000 player he had brought in to reinforce the reserves matching up against £37 million Luis Figo during the game.

Roberto Carlos has a now legendary reputation for the magnificent from dead ball situations with Exhibit A being his physics-defying bending effort for Brazil in Le Tournoi in 1997. In Madrid's obligatory training session at Elland Road the night before the match he had smashed a seat in the stadium's Kop end due to the ferocity of his shot. He was presented with an attempt 30 yards out and central to Robinson's goal but smashed his effort wide as his assault on the Elland Road furniture extended to the South Stand. Upon seeing that Madrid's pressure was increasing more and more the home crowd found their voices again in an attempt to give their troops a boost. But United's resistance was finally broken on 66 minutes. Figo forced Robinson into conceding a corner and from that, a quick give and go between Figo and Raul resulted in the former crossing into the far post where Hierro rose highest and headed the visitors in front. In a flash, it was a game, set, and match for Madrid. Carlos drove forward from left-back and played forward up his line to McManaman who then found Guti whose quick and decisive pass pierced the Leeds defence and found Raul who had perfectly timed his run to beat the offside trap and converted a simple finish home to extend the lead to an unassailable two.

It was from that point all over as a contest too. The remaining quarter of the game came and went without any further major chances for either team. Leeds tried in vain to force their way back into the game winning a small collection of free-kicks and corners which all came to nothing as Madrid professionally saw the remaining minutes out to claim the three points. It wasn't the complete humbling that Madrid's great rivals Barcelona had dished out to O'Leary's young side on the opening night of the previous group but there was a clear gulf in all departments between Leeds United and Real Madrid on the night.

Matteo later reflected on the game in his autobiography that Leeds was left "chasing shadows for 90 minutes" and that it was a "real footballing lesson and our fans knew it, as they showed by applauding the Madrid boys from the field at the final whistle". Matteo was subsequently chosen at random to complete UEFA's mandatory drug doping test post-match and was left in a room along the corridor of the Elland Road tunnel alone with Fernando Hierro. Remembering the Madrid team's fondness for a drink he took this opportunity to mingle with something stronger than coffee and collected a crate of beer from the player's lounge which the pair shared before continuing the drinks back at the Oulton Hotel.

David O'Leary was also of the opinion that his side was taught a lesson. "It was disappointing to lose my unbeaten home record as a manager in European competition, but if it had to go, the pain was eased by losing it to a side as talented as Real. There are times in football when you have to hold your hands up and say you've been outplayed, and a side of high-quality players outclassed us. I've never seen an average player in a Real Madrid shirt and the current crop contains some wonderful stars", he reflected.

Elsewhere on the night, Anderlecht saw off Lazio 1-0 to throw the cat amongst the pigeons in Group D and it was clear that Leeds would need something comparatively remarkable to their great escape from the first group phase if they were to progress any further. If they wanted an invite to the European party next season, they would also need a marked improvement domestically starting with a visit from Arsene Wenger's Arsenal.

When in Rome

Lazio 0-1 Leeds United

UEFA Champions League, Second Group Phase, Matchday Two

There has always been a healthy respect between Leeds United and Arsenal. Leeds had enjoyed 1-0 victories over the Gunners in their only two domestic cup successes at Wembley securing the League Cup in 1968 and The FA Cup in 1972. Sandwiched between those triumphs, Arsenal pipped Leeds to the 1970-71 league championship to form half of their double-winning campaign. But since Arsenal's record appearance holder David O'Leary took over the Elland Road dug-out there was some needle developing between the two sides and a fiery encounter on November 26th was no different. Eight bookings were shared (six from the visitors) as a deflected Oliver Dacourt free-kick on 56 minutes gave Leeds a much-needed three points and ensured there was no hangover from the defeat to Real Madrid. Rio Ferdinand was unveiled and paraded pre-match holding aloft his number 29 shirt to the Elland Road crowd. Rio saw potential in his new club and the opportunity to learn from his new boss when he spoke to the press. "I am pleased to be joining such an ambitious club. European football is what I need, and I want that and Leeds United can offer me that. This is a big step forward for me. The manager's former playing role was another big factor for me. He was a world-class centre half and has a lot to offer me". On the back of the record-breaking transfer, the silly season was in full flow as rumours floated that Leeds was linked with an audacious move for Brazilian phenomenon Ronaldo. Peter Ridsdale was quick to nip those rumours in the bud quickly stating, "There's more chance of Pele being in our team to play Leicester on Saturday". The world's most expensive defender wasn't signed in time to make the squad for the clash with the

Gunners but would have to wait until the following week when Leeds travelled to Filbert Street for the clash with Leicester City. Leicester's former home was somewhat of a bogey ground for Leeds at the time having lost in six out of their last seven visits. With the arrival of Ferdinand alongside the fit again Jonathan Woodgate and Lucas Radebe, O'Leary opted to ditch his usual 4-4-2 formation and try out the trio making a three-man central defensive backline. "Right now, the three of them give me plenty of alternative ways of playing. I like the idea of a 3-4-1-2 for instance – that plays to our strength. What I don't like is playing three at the back with wingbacks. Mostly I like to play with four at the back and with our players that is probably a 4-3-3 line-up. That gives us the stability at the back but plenty of attacking options as well. But we do have the flexibility and the ability to switch things when we think it's appropriate", O'Leary explained. The three-man defence plan had backfired explosively though as Leeds found themselves 3-0 down within the first half an hour thanks to three headed goals by Robbie Savage, Ade Akinbiyi, and Gerry Taggart. Things got worse for Leeds when Radebe was sent off on 66 minutes but some good news at least for United was that Harry Kewell came off the bench to make his first appearance of the season. The visiting ten men rallied in the final half hour with a goal from Mark Viduka proceeding Dacourt hitting a post and Kewell coming close to marking his return with a goal. It counted for nothing though as they suffered their sixth league defeat of the season.

Next up for Leeds though was another adventure into Europe as they returned to Italy to face Lazio. S.S. Lazio abbreviation for Società Sportiva Lazio presented yet another formidable opponent for Leeds to contend with. English fans would be familiar with the club as the team Paul Gascoigne departed England for in 1991 and were runners-up to compatriots Inter Milan in the 1998 UEFA Cup. The Italian flag - 'Scuduetto' - was proudly worn on their current shirts as they won the Serie A title in 1999/00 pipping Juventus by one point on the final day of the season. Their fortunes had turned thanks to large investment into their playing squad acquiring world stars such as Juan Sebastian Veron, Diego Simeone, Alessandro Nesta, and future Ballon D'or winner Pavel Nedved. Leading their attack was Argentine Hernan Crespo who became the world's second most expensive player after Luis Figo when he transferred from Parma for €56.81 million. Their head coach was also of great interest to English football supporters. Sven Goran Eriksson had won 18 major trophies in his club career and football news was dominated by the fact The Football Association opted for the unprecedented approach of appointing the Swedish coach as the man to replace Kevin Keegan as England manager – the first time a foreigner was given the role. Eriksson was due to begin his duties with England following the conclusion of his Lazio contract at the end of the 2000-01 season on a lucrative five-and-a-half-year contract. However, their title defence domestically was proving a struggle going into the Leeds game in 7th place in Serie A.

Lazio's home stadium was becoming familiar surroundings for Leeds United's team and supporters. The Stadio Olimpico is shared between Lazio and their fierce rivals AS Roma. Leeds had been drawn with Roma in their previous two UEFA Cup campaigns meaning this was United's third consecutive season where they travelled to the eternal city and its modern-day Colosseum. It was the first of these encounters in October 1998 which sealed O'Leary's full-time appointment as manager after he took caretaker charge of a pleasing performance that saw Leeds narrowly edged out 1-0 before another brave display in the return leg at Elland Road resulted in a goalless draw and elimination in the second round. A season later they went one better. A 0-0 draw in Rome followed by a superb 1-0 victory thanks to a Harry Kewell goal booked Leeds a place in the quarter-finals and made Europe stand up and take notice of O'Leary's emerging young side. The goalless draw in March 2000 was most memorable for a fantastic performance from goalkeeper Nigel Martyn in what must go down as his finest hour in the Leeds goal that he was later voted as the best to occupy in the club's history. Martyn still out from injury would not be making this trip, however. Olivier Dacourt was not yet part of the Leeds United setup for those games with Roma, but he had played a curious game at the Stadio Olimpico before. Whilst on national service for France in 1995 he represented his homeland in a World Cup for the military in which France defeated Italy 1-0. It was also the first of two trips to Rome in quick succession for captain Lucas Radebe. A week later 'The Chief' would receive a FIFA Fair Play award for his work against racism and his tireless work with children back in his homeland of Soweto in South Africa.

Already the game between Lazio and Leeds was shaping up to be an important one on Matchday Two of Group D. Both teams tasted defeat in their group openers and for Leeds in particular, avoiding defeat seemed essential as it was the last game before European football took its annual sabbatical before the competition re-commenced in February. A defeat would leave Leeds well adrift and a mountainous task for when they return to European action. On the other hand, a positive result would stand them in good stead with the break promising the return of experienced injured players such as David Batty and Nigel Martyn.

The return of Harry Kewell from his long injury layoff was as important as it was timely for Leeds. The Australian winger was arguably the most outrageous talent in the Leeds squad with pace and skills that wowed supporters and caused opposition problems. Since breaking through the FA Youth Cup winning side of 1997 and making his first team debut at the age of 17, Kewell became one of the hottest young talents in world football and won the PFA Young Player of the Year in 1999/00 and attracted a £25 million bid from Inter Milan that was rejected by Leeds before injury prevented him playing any part in their Champions League campaign to date. He also provided the Leeds squad with some much-needed tension relief on the afternoon of the Lazio game. The squad was spending some downtime stretching their legs whilst walking around a local zoo when the Australian visited a shop and purchased a leather jacket for his partner - Emmerdale actress Sheree Murphy. Kewell had thought the jacket cost a few hundred - small change for a Premier League footballer, but he was confused by the conversion rate and only noticed when he checked the receipt back on the team bus that the jacket had cost him £20,000. He persuaded the coach driver to pull over and sprint to return his partner's gift for which he received an ambush of playful jibes from his amused teammates.

Kewell would only be fit enough to make the substitutes bench on a wet night in Rome whereas Lazio had injury doubts over defender Nesta and midfielder Veron but the pair both made the starting line-up. Ferdinand had travelled with the team but was ineligible to play until after the winter break, so O'Leary had opted to revert to his usual 4-4-2 formation with a centre-back pairing of Woodgate and Radebe. Woodgate was made the scapegoat for the horror show of a first half at Filbert Street and suffered the indignity of being substituted before the half-time whistle. Importantly too for Leeds was the eligibility of Oliver Dacourt in the midfield after serving his suspension as he was a blatant miss in the game against Real Madrid.

There was a crowd of only 42,450 making up just over half of the 70,634 capacity of the Stadio Olimpico. Yet that did nothing to diminish an intimidating atmosphere for the visitors to contend with as the Leeds bus was targeted by home supporters on mopeds driving alongside, hitting it with large sticks and once the game had got underway every touch from a man in yellow was greeted by loud jeers on another wet European night. There was a relatively small contingent of traveling Leeds fans compared to those they took to Barcelona and Milan. In the previous season, Leeds had taken approximately 6,000 fans to the same stadium for their Last 16 UEFA Cup tie with Roma but a mixture of Christmas being on the horizon, the expensive nature of what was already their fifth European visit that season, and a will to save the pennies for an unmissable trip to Real Madrid and the Bernabéu coming up the following March contributed to Leeds taking just under a thousand fans for this game.

Showing Leeds was up for the fight though, Mark Viduka received an early booking for catching Nesta with an elbow and on replays it can be said was lucky to escape further punishment, but the tempo was set by the Australian. Leeds made an impressive start to the game and a Lee Bowyer free-kick across the face of goal avoided everyone including the diving efforts of Viduka, then Alan Smith, and finally Woodgate at the back post. As the visitors continued to play the role of the protagonist in the first half, Viduka continued being a nuisance up front giving his marker Fernando Couto a hard time. They came agonisingly close to opening the scoring from a Lee Bowyer corner. Erik Bakke rose highest to meet the delivery and headed towards the bottom corner however Lazio were thankful they had former Crystal Palace midfielder Attilio Lombardo on the back post to hook the ball off the line.

Lazio's first real attack on the Leeds goal came from an in-swinging Veron corner which was hit with pace and flew past Paul Robinson into the back post where Guiseppe Pancardo hit the crossbar from a yard out. Leeds struggled to clear the danger until eventually, Veron's shot cleared the crossbar. Lazio came close again shortly after when a deep cross from Pavel Nedved was teased into the six-yard box where Hernan Crespo got in between two Leeds defenders but couldn't connect for what would have been a certain goal but for a vital touch from Woodgate. The defender's important intervention went unnoticed by the referee Claude Colombo and a goal kick instead of a corner was given. Woodgate was again the hero when he cleared a goal-bound diving header from Marcelo Salas - which had beaten Robinson - off the line with his head. Leeds had the chance to take a lead into the break in first-half stoppage time. Some neat build-up play resulted in Bakke playing in Viduka who shimmied and turned to leave Nesta and then Pancardo on the floor before playing a ball into the back post which found Bowyer unattended from any defenders, but his lunging effort went just wide.

Despite the positive performance, the visitor's dressing room was animated as O'Leary accused Dominic Matteo of deliberately trying to injure an opponent to which Matteo took exception. An argument ensued during which the hero of Milan was dismissed from the dressing room, and he proceeded to take his boots off thinking that was the end of his involvement on the night before being told he would still be needed for the second half by United's coaches. "Afterwards I did apologise to David for how I reacted – even though I still thought his accusation was wrong. I was expecting him to do the same, but he didn't. That annoyed me at the time, but the most annoying part of our row was that it had all been so unnecessary", Matteo later reflected in his autobiography.

The first chance of the second half saw Lucas Radebe force the dangerous Nedved into narrowing his angle for a shot into the side netting and Leeds's next chance saw Dacourt try his luck from range which went narrowly over the crossbar. The Frenchman fancied his chances after scoring his first Leeds goal against Arsenal and hitting the woodwork at Filbert Street a few days earlier. Midway through the second half, Nedved again looked most likely to make something happen for the home side. He managed to turn away from Bakke and unleash a strike on goal which went just wide of the target.

Mark Viduka was enjoying what he would later describe as his best-ever performance in a Leeds shirt- even above the four-goal show against Liverpool. He came close to marking it with a goal. Alan Smith attempted a cross which was blocked by the left-back and looked to be going out for a corner but instead bounced backward to Lee Bowyer who played an inviting cross into Viduka who struck first time from six yards but an intervention from Lombardo took the venom off the shot and was denied by goalkeeper Luca Marchegiani as he parried over. Woodgate then came close to rounding off his impressive restorative performance with a strike that went wide when he forayed forward from an attacking throw-in but was closed down quickly by Nesta. At the other end, a long-lofted ball from Simeone bypassed the Leeds back line and presented Crespo with a one-on-one with Robinson but the keeper was quick off his line and prevented Crespo from lifting the ball over him.

With 10 minutes to go came the breakthrough. Kewell – who replaced Jason Wilcox on 70 minutes - attracted two Lazio defenders on the left-hand side with a quick foot ploy and played in Smith outside the Lazio box. Smith outstretched his right leg to play a first-time pass into Viduka. who held the ball with his first touch and his second was a magnificent nonchalant no-look backheel with Couto on his back and played into the path of Smith who had carried on his run. Smith puffed his cheeks, composed himself and passed the ball past Marchegiani and into the net. It was Smith's ninth goal of the season but only the first time he netted in twelve games. This, perhaps alongside his goal that secured qualification in Munich was his most important yet and in hindsight his golden moment for the club. But the aesthetics of the goal was a culmination of a blossoming strike partnership that had been forming over recent weeks between Smith and Viduka. It was another example that Smith – raw and rough around the edges – was coming of age. After a second underwhelming season followed his impressive breakthrough season there were suggestions in the summer that he was on the verge of a move to Manchester City. But he had a big supporter in his manager. "Alan was only 17 when he first came into the team two seasons ago and did a great job. Last season I have to admit that he had a bad one. A lot of people were willing to jump on his back, but I wasn't one of them. I am a big believer in him", O'Leary told Don Warters. As for his partnership with Viduka, Smith praised his more senior partner for his part in the pairing. "I was disappointed when Jimmy Floyd Hasselbaink left the club because I enjoyed playing alongside him. But Mark Viduka is the type of player I can play in partnership with. He's a good target man and he can hold the ball up so well but there's more to his game than that. He has two good feet and a keen eye for goal. We seem to be working well together", Smith also told Don Warters. There were plenty more impressive displays from Leeds players on the night and Jonathan Woodgate was singled out for praise from his manager and teammates days after being the scapegoat of the Leicester defeat.

Leeds showed maturity keeping possession wisely near Lazio's corner flag throughout three minutes of additional time and the final whistle was greeted by cheers from Leeds's travelling contingent. It was the first time Leeds had won in Italy in seven attempts after four draws and three defeats previously and for all their positivity in the Champions League so far, it was only their first victory in the competition since the 6-0 rout of Besiktas back in September. Italian Police had kept a contingent of Leeds fans situated high in the Curva Sud section of the arena and another sing-song like the one in Milan ensued with Leeds's conquering gladiators and their supporters in unison, with all the usual suspects involved and Rio Ferdinand initiating himself endearingly to the Leeds fans as he ditched, *I'm forever blowing bubbles* for *Marching on Together*.

The result would indirectly contribute to the chain reaction of Sven Goran accelerating his move to FA headquarters as he resigned from his post at Lazio to take over England earlier than expected a month later on January 9th. Eriksson saw first-hand some impressive auditions from Woodgate, Smith, and Robinson for the next England manager and praised his opponents post-match. "It's always embarrassing to lose but I don't think it is embarrassing to lose to a good side like Leeds United," he said.

From one incoming England manager to a former one - Glenn Hoddle who was watching in preparation for his Southampton team facing Leeds in their next match described the victory as "one of the greatest results in Europe from an English side in the last twenty years".

O'Leary had encouraged his team to be bold and go for the win when everyone else was suggesting a draw would be fine and he saluted his troops on another memorable evening on the continent saying, "I am delighted for the players in their learning process. It was lovely to win, and it gets us back into the group and we can put it to bed now until February. It just seems to get better and better. You think about Milan and what happened there and now we've been to another famous stadium and come away with a great result".

Elsewhere, Real Madrid thumped Anderlecht 4-1 which meant Leeds had moved up to 2nd place in Group D and in a qualification place but still level on points with the Belgians who they would meet in a double header when the competition re-commenced two months later. But even without European football for this period, life at Elland Road was never quiet and Leeds United would yet again be about to make the headlines on the front and back pages.

Leeds United on Trial

If the Champions League exploits felt like a dream for Leeds United then the Premier League had the nasty habit of bringing them back down to earth, like an early morning alarm clock awakening you from an unrealistically pleasant dream. Leeds's final trip to Southampton's rickety old stadium, The Dell, saw them fall to another Premier League defeat (1-0). O'Leary was disappointed not to capitalise on the momentum from the Lazio victory by taking the points at Southampton which he described as a less desirable place to do so. "Three points escaped us at Southampton in the competition which is most important as far as we are concerned. I would have preferred to have been somewhere like Old Trafford, the Stadium of Light, or Elland Road where there was a big game and a great atmosphere just to get the adrenaline going again", O'Leary commented in his next programme notes. Rio Ferdinand spoke for the first time since becoming a Leeds United player in the matchday programme for a home game with Sunderland and stated that he still thought Leeds could turn their domestic season around and challenge for the league title. Ferdinand's optimistic cry started well as Leeds bounced back with a 2-0 home win over Sunderland thanks to goals from Lee Bowyer and Mark Viduka in one of the more professional and routine performances in the league to date that season. Their cause was helped with O'Leary able to pick from the most available squad yet with Harry Kewell completing his first full game and David Batty making a welcome return as a 78th-minute substitute after twelve months out of action. The return of a mostly fit and healthy squad raised positivity among players and fans alike as Viduka added his thoughts on United returning to full strength. "We have had a lot of games so far this season and have been struggling with injuries.

We have had to chop and change and there has been a heavy workload for some of the players. But now with players coming back, we can start getting used to playing with a regular line-up. I have looked at our schedule and for the next month or two, it is very hectic. Even when the Christmas period is out of the way, there are a lot of games in a short time, so we know we have to string some results together. We know we can do it", stated the Australian striker. With players coming back and bolstering the squad, Matthew Jones went through the exit door in a £3.35 million move to Leicester City after finding opportunities to truly breakthrough at Elland Road sparse. Leeds's squad was strengthened further however by welcoming an exciting new signing in the form of Robbie Keane arriving on an initial loan until the end of the season from Inter Milan before signing a five-year deal in the summer of 2001 for £12 million – less than two months from his impromptu visit to the Leeds team at the San Siro in their pre-AC Milan training session. Leeds could have spared themselves that expense by signing the striker when he was on trial at Elland Road as a fourteen-year-old schoolboy when he joined a contingent of Irish schoolboys trying their luck, but despite scoring in a 3-0 win he was not asked to return. Keane, even at only 20 years of age, was well known to Premier League fans after impressing in a previous stint at Coventry City which earned him a move to the Italian giants but within six months his time at the San Siro was over. Keane had many admirers back in the Premier League and Leeds beat competition from Chelsea and Liverpool for his signature. With the hefty £1 million loan fee coming only a month after the club's record outlay for Ferdinand, Leeds topped the league table for deficits over the previous five years for Premier League clubs with their deficit totalling close to £50 million. Retrospectively, this was the beginning of the frivolous spending and chasing the dream that would eventually bring the club to its knees. The latest edition of Leeds United's in-house fan-written magazine *Leeds Leeds Leeds* carried the headline the 'loadsamoney issue' with Ferdinand as the cover star. O'Leary, like the fans, also had no objections to the spending on the squad. The Leeds manager had been repeatedly insisting that quality players were needed for him to progress the side ever since his promotion to the top job and here he was finally being backed aggressively in that department. However, the inconsistency his team was showing – particularly domestically – had frustrated him. "I am far from happy about our position. I don't want to manage a mid-table side and the players do not want to play in one – but taking the longer view, I think we have made solid progress in the last twelve months, and I expect that to continue", O'Leary stated.

Two days after signing, Keane made his debut as a substitute with 23 minutes remaining but couldn't prevent a 2-1 defeat at home to Aston Villa. Goals from George Boateng and Gareth Southgate (Elland Road proving a happy hunting ground for the future England manager) made Jonathan Woodgate's late goal nothing more than a consolation. United's glum festive season continued into Boxing Day as their Premier League programme reached the halfway stage with a trip to St. James's Park to face Newcastle. Despite taking the lead through an Olivier Dacourt free-kick, two goals in quick concession just before half-time from Nolberto Solano and Clarence Acuna turned the game in the host's favour. O'Leary stated that it was his team's "most disappointing performance" since he took charge of the team.

A chance to bounce back quickly disappeared as a trip to Everton three days later was postponed due to icy conditions so Leeds entered the new year in 14th place and closer to the drop zone than the European places in terms of position and points. They began 2001 with a home draw with Middlesbrough with Robbie Keane rescuing a point from the penalty spot for his first Leeds goal after Alen

Boskic had put Boro ahead. The FA Cup presented a chance for Leeds to get back on track against Division 1 side Barnsley in a Yorkshire derby. Mark Viduka had opened the scoring after just nine minutes, but Leeds couldn't put the tie to bed despite creating numerous first-half chances. In the second period, the underdogs threatened a replay or even a win with some incessant pressure, but Leeds held on to limp into the next round. A visit to Maine Road to face Manchester City came nearly a year to the day since the epic FA Cup clash where Leeds prevailed 5-2. Whilst that encounter had the billing of David and Goliath with the team's top of the Premier League and Division 1 respectively, City were now on equal ground in the Premier League and both teams entered the game in the lower reaches of the table. O'Leary was concerned that a defeat could drag his team into a relegation dogfight and told his players so before the game. Retrospectively speaking in his book *Leeds United on Trial* he stated. "In short, victory was nothing less than critical. The awareness that we could slide into trouble if we screwed up at Maine Road permeated the club. I was worried whether such a young group of players would cope with the pressures of a relegation battle. On the eve of the match, I dared to mention the dreaded 'R' word at my press conference. Relegation was an issue lurking on the horizon, and I felt the time had arrived for a few home truths". Erik Bakke had given Leeds a 31st-minute lead, but it was a tight encounter until Lee Bowyer brought some breathing space before two stoppage-time goals from substitute Keane created a handsome scoreline as Leeds claimed a 4-0 victory and a much-needed three points. Despite the victory easing some pressure, O'Leary was still in a frustrated yet philosophical mood. "Our league position is disgraceful, but we can come out stronger for this experience. This win will put us in a good heart, but we must build on it. If we do that, we can move on and be a threat again. But as a coach, this season has been unenjoyable", he said. A quick return visit from Bobby

Robson's Newcastle just 25 days after the Boxing Day clash on Tyneside brought another defeat however as the Magpies claimed a league double over Leeds with a 3-1 win.

***

A saga running in the background in January involved club captain Lucas Radebe. Radebe had an ongoing conflict of interests as a proud captain of both his club and his native South African national team. With Radebe now approaching his 32nd birthday and with a handful of injury issues that regularly halted his involvement over long periods, Leeds was keen to protect their skipper's heavy workload and a calendar that often saw his services double booked. On 4th January, Radebe signed a three-year contract extension until the summer of 2004 with improved terms. The length of the contract also ensured he would be promised a testimonial at the end of the deal due to spending a decade at Elland Road. Radebe's signing was a boost for Leeds in terms of tying down an asset who often attracted admiring glances from rival would-be suitors but was also a welcome one for Radebe himself whose place in the team had been under threat since the arrival of Rio Ferdinand. But the club versus country war would not go away. The day after signing his new contract Radebe asked the South African FA to withdraw from an African Nations Cup qualifier against Mauritius as it coincided with Leeds's trip to face Manchester City. Radebe's agent Gary Blumberg stated at the time: "Lucas is trying to pace himself in regard to call-ups. I don't think they will have any problem winning that game (v Mauritius) so South Africa can be more liberal with team selection". However, Radebe did put country before club later in the month when after a shock 1-1 draw with Mauritius, South Africa insisted on his participation in a World Cup qualifier against Burkina Faso on the same day Leeds was due to host Liverpool in an FA

Cup match. Leeds was restricted by FIFA rules where South Africa had the power to demand he be released from his club for international duty. On 23rd January Radebe announced his retirement from international football to focus on his Leeds United career. Predictably, the South African party was keen to change his mind and the chief of the South African FA, Danny Jordaan, met Leeds club officials to thrash out a compromise. It was decided that Leeds would have the first call on their player's availability when domestic and international games coincide and Radebe would be able to continue playing for 'Bafana Bafana' when Leeds were not scheduled to play. It meant Radebe would not be available to represent his country for their upcoming qualifiers against Malawi and Guinea which conflicted with Leeds's upcoming fixture with Tottenham Hotspur and their preparation for hosting Lazio later in March.

***

A trip to Villa Park to face Aston Villa wasn't an ideal game for O'Leary's side to remedy their wounds from the Newcastle loss. Villa had come out victorious in the previous four meetings between the sides and took the lead through a Paul Merson goal. Bowyer equalised shortly after though and Ian Harte secured the three points on the road with the winner fifteen minutes from time. The reward for the third-round FA Cup win over Barnsley was a home tie with Liverpool who had become one of Leeds's greatest rivals in terms of league positions and shopping in the same player pool in the transfer market. This cup tie was closely fought and looked to be heading to an Anfield replay before late, late goals from Nick Barmby and Emile Heskey sent Leeds packing as the Reds went on to win the FA Cup.

Leeds United however had bigger worries than cup elimination once the weekend was over. The trial involving predominately Lee Bowyer and Jonathan

Woodgate, but also involving Michael Duberry and reserve team player Tony Hackworth was originally scheduled for the close season in the summer of 2001. However, a reschedule meant that the cloud that had been hanging over Elland Road in the background for just over twelve months would finally burst as the trial began on 29th January 2001 amidst the middle of a season in which Leeds were chasing their tail in the Premier League and had a Champions League campaign to pick up just a couple of weeks later. To recap, Bowyer, Woodgate and Hackworth were charged with causing grievous bodily harm to Sarfraz Najeib along with two of Woodgate's friends Paul Clifford and Neale Caveney whilst Duberry was charged with conspiracy to pervert the course of justice for his role in the aftermath of the attack. O'Leary was staunch in his views and was not willing to put himself in a position to protect his players should they be found guilty. "I told my players before the trial began on 29th January that if they had chased and brutally kicked a person, whatever the circumstances, they deserved to go to prison as a punishment" he said. However, it was revealed that Bowyer and Woodgate would be available for selection throughout the trial. Peter Ridsdale was quiet ahead of the trial saying: "It is entirely up to the manager, but if selected there is no reason why they could not play. Of course, they would not be training with the rest of the squad, but they will be able to maintain their fitness levels in the evenings. David O'Leary will assess those and how they are psychologically before making his own decision on a match-by-match basis". Carole Seheult – a clinical psychologist - was interviewed explaining that she thought that it was unlikely the players involved would be able to sustain their performance levels throughout the trial. Whereas Bowyer remained a mainstay in the team, Woodgate would not feature again in the season, being named as an unused substitute five times. O'Leary stated in *Leeds United on Trial* that Woodgate rarely reported into training during the trial and was not in the mental or physical state for selection regardless. "On the few occasions, he did show up at our training ground, I realised we couldn't even consider him for match action. He looked like a ghost. The weight and muscle had dropped off him. He was completely shot through", he said of Woodgate. An injury was announced via the press, but it had become clear that was a smokescreen for the defender's absence.

Despite the distraction, Bowyer started in a home league game over Coventry City two days after the start of the trial which was won 1-0 via a splendid goal from an overhead kick from Keane who was beginning to find his feet at Elland Road. O'Leary praised Bowyer's performance speaking post-match, "He doesn't let you down and I am just grateful that we don't have to pay him by the mile with the distances he covers in the course of a match". A 2-1 win at Portman Road over high-flying, newly promoted, Ipswich Town followed thanks to goals from Viduka and Keane. It was the first time Leeds had won three consecutive games in the league that season and suddenly they were propelled up to sixth place, just five points behind third-place Liverpool, as January turned to February. There was the possible route of the Intertoto Cup – a summer competition where entry had to be applied for and access granted to the highest-place finishers in the European domestic leagues (below the allotted European qualifying places) battling it out for a place in the UEFA Cup. O'Leary had revealed that the club was looking at applying for the competition as a back-up but the normal route for European qualification was the desired outcome. "I would like to spend a holiday with my family. Believe me in this job you need a break. You need to have time away from the players, who are sick to death of me for eleven months of the year. I wouldn't like to be spending June with them", he said.

The postponed trip to Goodison Park to face Everton was re-arranged for February 7th. The Wednesday night fixture on Merseyside provided a logistical nightmare if O'Leary was to include Lee Bowyer in his squad following a full day on trial at Hull Crown Court. A helicopter was chartered to ensure the midfielder made the 128-mile distance in time to make the match. Leeds's winning run was halted with a 2-2 draw, but it was a useful point for Leeds after twice coming from behind to secure a point with goals from Viduka and Olivier Dacourt - scoring on his return to his old club. In the final game before the resumption of the Champions League, Derby County held Leeds to a goalless draw for the second season running. The point though did ensure Leeds had reached the 40-point mark, the bare minimum magic mark relieving any of O'Leary's earlier pessimism about relegation and Leeds had wrestled themselves instead into European qualification contention from being stranded in mid-table. Next up was a visit from Anderlecht as the Champions League picked up where it left off and after United's heroic win in Rome, it was all to play for.

Brussels Rout

Vs Anderlecht (Home and Away)

Champions League Second Group Phase, Matchdays 3 and 4.

Upon the resumption of European competition, Group D in the second group phase was beginning to mirror Group H in the first phase for Leeds in the way that it was structured. Whereas Leeds was given a footballing lesson from Barcelona in the first game and responded with a brilliant win against AC Milan at Elland Road, this time round they had been soundly beaten by Real Madrid before recovering to record a famous win in Rome against Lazio. Leeds had put themselves in pole position to progress with a double header against Besiktas – considered the most enviable of the three group opponents – in the first stage that yielded four points. And now back-to-back games against Anderlecht looked to be key games in which to pick up points against a team with less household names than Madrid and Lazio who were themselves battling out their own double header. Leeds and Anderlecht were both locked on three points with the English side above on goal difference. Both teams had defeated Lazio 1-0 but the fact that Madrid had beaten Anderlecht 4-1 back in December meant Leeds went into the ties in second place. Unusually for Leeds, they had the luxury of no weekend distraction between the two face-offs with the Belgians due to a gap in their domestic schedule for an FA Cup weekend in which they were no longer in because of their fourth-round defeat to Liverpool whereas Anderlecht faced a visit to KRC Harelbeke in their pursuit for the Belgian league title.

Anderlecht, also a club of Royal Decree like Real Madrid – members of the Société Royale and allowed to wear a crown as part of their club emblem – is the main club from the Belgian capital of Brussels. They were enjoying a dominant spell in their homeland claiming their 25th league title in 1999/00 and were top of the Belgian Pro League going into the clashes with Leeds. 'The Mauves' had built a formidable fortress at their Constant Vanden Stock Stadion home winning their past 21 domestic home games as well as their last nine European home ties with victims as illustrious as Manchester United and Lazio, pipping the English side to first place in the first group phase.

The Brussels club had enjoyed continued European success in the late 1970's and early 80's lifting the European Cup Winners Cup in 1976 – defeating West Ham United 4-2. They were beaten in the final of the same competition a year later falling to a 2-0 defeat to German side Hamburg but went on to regain the trophy in 1978 beating Austria Vienna 4-0 in the final. They subsequently defeated the all-conquering Liverpool team of the time in the Super Cup. They won the UEFA Cup in 1983 beating Benfica and would have retained the trophy the next year but for a defeat to Tottenham Hotspur on penalties in the final.

Leeds and Anderlecht's paths had crossed 26 years earlier in 1975 in the quarter-finals of the European Cup. In 2001 they would again be playing out a double header that would likely decide who would progress to the last eight of Europe's elite after Lazio's poor start to life in Group D weakened their own chances of progression. In 1975 the first leg was in serious doubt of being played and a postponement seemed likely due to thick fog in West Yorkshire, but East German referee Rudi Glockner allowed the game to go ahead. The white shirts of Leeds perhaps went undetected as they raced into a 2-0 lead before half-time. Firstly, Joe Jordan put United ahead after nine minutes although a large section of the 43,195 crowd couldn't even see the goal for the fog. Chants of "Tell us who scored" were sung until Jordan was announced as the goal scorer by the PA announcer. That goal was followed by a headed goal from Gordon McQueen. The game was notable as the first-time inspirational captain Billy Bremner was substituted when he was replaced by Terry Yorath - such was manager Jimmy Armfield's assurance that his team was in control - and the tie was as good as won when Peter Lorimer rounded the game off by adding a third a minute from full-time. Bremner gave the perfect reaction to his substitution in the second leg two weeks later when he was the match-winner as Leeds triumphed 1-0 in Brussels. A 4-0 on aggregate win eased them into a semi-final showdown with Barcelona.

Back to 2001, first up was the meeting at Elland Road on 13th February. David O'Leary was wary of the importance of the two games coming up and the stern challenge that awaited his side." There may be a few people who are thinking that we went to Rome and beat Lazio so Anderlecht should create no problems. If they are, I'm here to tell them to think again. I've seen Anderlecht play and they are a very good footballing side. Their strength is going forward, so I think we are in for an entertaining game", he said. Among the players to watch were Anderlecht's little and large strike pairing of 6ft 8 Jan Koller and 5'10 Thomas Radzinski whereas 22-year-old Belgian midfielder Walter Baseggio had been compared to United's Lee Bowyer.

Bowyer had only narrowly made the team to start the game after standing trial at Hull Crown court throughout the day of the match and made the 70-mile dash to arrive just in time; around 6:30 pm to be included for the 7:45 pm kick-off. The court case ensured that Bowyer would only be available for Leeds's home European ties and considering he and Jonathan Woodgate (who was named on the bench) had missed two weeks of training they had nowhere near the preparation needed for a big Champions League match.

The near six-week hiatus of European football was not only useful for Leeds regaining some much-needed consistency in the Premier League, but it allowed key players to return from injury and O'Leary's side had a lot more of a senior look to it. Paul Robinson had performed wonders in goal, but the return of Nigel Martyn gave more experience to the young team as did the return of the prodigal son David Batty who was starting to form a productive partnership with Oliver Dacourt in the centre of midfield which would grace the European stage for the first time. It wasn't just the starting eleven that had a stronger look. In previous games such as the AC Milan game at the San Siro, such was the inexperience of the Leeds substitutes, David O'Leary went against making changes despite several players playing with knocks. Now the Leeds manager could call upon some depth with players such as Woodgate, Erik Bakke, Jason Wilcox, and Harry Kewell in reserve to call upon for reinforcements.

Rio Ferdinand was also eligible to make his first Champions League appearance in his 15th game since signing for Leeds. "I am really looking forward to the Anderlecht game because everything about the Champions League seems to be so much better than anything else. It's the music we come out to as much as anything. You can play Champions League on the computer or just watch a game on the TV and the music really sets the mood. It is so good. Everything about this competition is a different class so it will be great to be a part of it. It is one of the main reasons why I came to the club because playing in something like this is what we all dream about", the record transfer man said to the matchday programme.

Ineligible for the game though was Robbie Keane whose previous representation in the competition for Inter Milan earlier in the season left him cup-tied. The Irishman had made an impressive start to his Leeds career scoring six goals in eight starts. It was just as well that Keane had hit the ground running as goals were in short supply from Leeds's usual front two. Mark Viduka had failed to find the net in his last eight games whilst Alan Smith's winner at Lazio was his only goal in his last 26 appearances. O'Leary defended his strikers ahead of the game from criticism from some sections of the supporters. "It's typical of the short-term view taken by people who don't appreciate how football really is. You have to remember that this is Mark's first season in the Premiership down here and his overall contribution has been first-class", he said to Don Warters. The manager also encouraged Smith to take his opportunity with Keane out of the team. "I want Alan to come in and give me a selection problem", he said.

The opening stages of the first game at Elland Road was cagy with both sides knowing the importance of the two games ahead of them in deciding who will most likely follow Real Madrid into the quarter-finals and it was a particularly nervy start from Leeds on a damp night in West Yorkshire. Anderlecht should have drawn first blood in the first half. Bertrand Crasson played in a cross from the corner point of the 18-yard box which attempted to find Koller who was lurking from six yards out, but he missed his cue. However, the ball did evade Martyn and Ferdinand behind Koller, and the ball just bobbled over Bart Goor's foot as he dived feet first to turn into an empty net - similar to the famous chance for Paul Gascoigne for England against Germany in the semi-final of Euro 96. Leeds was given an early let-off.

Leeds showed their teeth for the first time with a long-range shot from Ian Harte's powerful left foot, but it was watched all the way by the goalkeeper Zvonko Milojevic. Then Viduka came close to breaking his duck after Smith had chested down a deep cross from Harte and played in the Australian who set his sights on goal only for Milojevic to save to his left-hand post and tip the ball round for a corner to Leeds. At the other end, Martyn needed to stop Yves Vanderhaeghe's shot just outside the box after some neat play by Anderlecht, but the two teams went into the half-time break goalless.

Leeds knew the merit of winning all three points in the second period, such was Anderlecht's impressive home form for the return meeting a week later, a draw at Elland Road was likely to mean an advantage to the Belgians, so Leeds needed to make this game count. They had the first chance of the second half when Dacourt gained possession adjacent to the centre circle and played out to the wide left to Dominic Matteo, who's cross into the penalty area evaded Smith but reached Viduka - who with his back to goal turned and shot but couldn't get a meaningful contact with the ball and it was gathered easily by Mllojevic.

The home crowd were given a lift on 53 minutes when Matteo was replaced by Harry Kewell for his first Champions League appearance at Elland Road. Straight away he made an impact, frightening Anderlecht's right back Crasson with his direct running and pace before unleashing the best shot off the night so far, forcing Milojevic into a save. But disaster struck for Leeds on 65 minutes as they fell behind. From a free-kick in a defensive position, Koller used his towering frame to block Ferdinand and cushion the ball into Alin Stoica, 25 yards from goal. Stoica played a clever one-two with Goor which penetrated the Leeds defence and the Romanian international carried on his run and passed the ball past Martyn. The majority of the Elland Road crowd was stunned into silence except for the Belgian contingent in the 'cheese wedge' corner of the stadium where one of the biggest European followings at Leeds that season was celebrating with their team.

The goal sparked a reaction from Leeds however and within ten minutes they were back level. Bowyer won a free-kick from Vanderhaeghe 30 yards from goal. Harte stood over the free-kick with clear intentions on goal rather than a cross as he twice glanced up at Milojevic's goal. After a long run-up, the Irishman struck his shot low and with pace swerving past the Anderlecht defensive wall and into the bottom corner. After a lull from falling behind, the atmosphere was ignited again, and Leeds had their tails up sensing they could win the game. But they almost fell behind again from an Anderlecht break as Goor's cross from the wide left was hanging across the Leeds goal and was missed by Martyn and found Koller at the back post. The Czech's effort was made more difficult as it bounced just as he was about to strike though, and he couldn't adjust his long legs appropriately enough and skied the ball over an empty goalframe. Leeds breathed a sigh of relief but with just three minutes of normal time remaining it was a case of cometh the hour, cometh the man. A misjudgement on a bounce from centre-back Glen De Boeck from a punt forward from Martyn was capitalised by Smith who played into a vacant space left by the Anderlecht defence. Onrushing into the box was the tireless Bowyer. Leeds's number 11- despite his complete lack of match preparation and having spent the day in court – somehow found the energy to finish his run past the opposition's defence. His first touch looked to have widened his angle, but his right-footed shot arrowed through the legs of Milojevic and into the far corner. Bowyer's liberty was at risk and his reputation was on the line over at Hull Crown Court, but it was clear he was popular at Elland Road as he celebrated screaming into the Kop end. Leeds had turned it around after staring defeat in the face with just a third of the game to go.

Two minutes of added time were indicated, and Leeds needed to see out a free-kick from 35 yards. Stoica lofted it into the crowded penalty area where

Kewell headed away, only for it to land at Radzinski – looking to add to his tally of five Champions League goals so far - whose instinctive effort was goal bound before Martyn dived low to preserve a precious victory for the whites.

Loud whistles encouraged referee Karl-Erik Nilsson to blow his own and when he did a roar from the crowd and a beaming smile with outstretched arms from O'Leary indicated the importance of the victory for Leeds. Bowyer had been used to hearing echoes of "Bowyer's going down" for over a year during away games from teasing opposition fans but innocent until proven guilty was the take from the majority of Leeds United's supporters and chants of "Lee Bowyer, Lee Bowyer" rang around the stadium in a show of appreciation for their controversial star. Bowyer's energy to make that run and match-winning finish so deep into an elite-level match with so little preparation was remarkable and even more so considering the midfielder's off-the-pitch way of living. Eddie Gray described him in his autobiography as "one of football's freaks". "Managers and coaches are always stressing the importance of players training hard and eating the right food, but their arguments – all perfectly sound – are liable to collapse when you look at Lee. His diet is not exactly what you would expect from a highly-tuned athlete. On European trips you immediately know that the town or city has a McDonald's outlet by the cheer that emanates from the back of the bus when it passes one", he said. The assistant manager also added that football in this period was a form of escapism for Bowyer from his off-pitch struggles. "A lot of people were amazed by Lee's performances, given the strain of the court case. But he looked upon playing for Leeds as an escape from those pressures. Our matches and particularly our European ties, provided an outlet for all the stress he was experiencing off the field, and I think that was one of the reasons why his physical contribution was so high", wrote Gray. It can be argued that Bowyer's performances throughout Leeds's Champions League campaign were talismanic and the late winner to secure all three points against Anderlecht was the most important yet. Such were his performances throughout the season he would go on to win the player's player of the year award at the end of the season securing 90% of the vote. Among the voters for the indefatigable Bowyer was Olivier Dacourt. "I picked Lee Bowyer! It was because of the whole trial affair… 95, maybe 97per cent of players would be sick and be unable to play. You never forget that he never trained with us – just played the games. Nobody could do that. He can run all day. So just for that, the pressure and everything, every day in court, then coming to the games in the night and often scoring… it was Lee Bowyer for me", the French midfielder later told Leeds, Leeds, Leeds magazine.

Dominic Matteo continued his hobby of socialising with his European opponents' post-match when he invited Jan Koller and Thomas Radzinski out for a few pints at the Majestyk nightclub but on the eve of Valentine's Day, there was no love lost between the two clubs after Anderlecht manager Aime Antheunis spoke to the press. "Leeds are not a good side, I was not impressed by them. Next week in Brussels will be a different game. We will see what happens then. How can a home team create so few chances and win the game? One-nil is the right result, 1-1 just about acceptable". He wasn't finished there either as he continued his rant to the Belgian press in the build-up to the return meeting. It was a typical show of arrogance that Anderlecht had come to be renowned for in European football quarters. Leeds United's Director of Public Relations and Corporate Affairs David Walker revealed in *Leeds Leeds Leeds magazine* that the Anderlecht arrogance extended to the boardroom also. A 1-1 draw would have suited the Belgians before they inevitably disposed of United in Brusells was the viewpoint discussed on the eve of the

Elland Road clash at UEFA's customary pre-match delegation lunch. "We have beaten Manchester United and every other team that has visited our stadium so you will not be a problem for us" quipped one official. Bowyer's late intervention had modified those plans ahead of the return meeting a week later.

***

Whilst Leeds United was enjoying a rare weekend off Anderlecht kept up their league title defence with a 4-1 win over KRC Harelbeke. It was an angry Leeds team that they would have to turn their attention to for this vital Matchday 4 in Group D though, incensed by Aime Antheunis's comments and the perceived arrogance of the Belgian team. The Anderlecht's manager's comments were translated from French to English to the Leeds squad by Oliver Dacourt and as the cliche goes, those words were 'hung on the dressing room wall'. Antheunis's comments had irked his counterpart in O'Leary but what they did do was make his team talk a whole lot easier ahead of the clash in Brussels. Retrospectively speaking, O'Leary admitted that the comments and disrespect from a team they had defeated had been a motivating factor, but that Leeds needed to do their talking on the pitch by beating them fair and square. Antheunis did eventually back-track before the game saying this would actually be his team's hardest game of the season, but the damage was already done in galvanising the Leeds United squad.

Leeds hardly needed extra motivation anyway as eight days after the Elland Road clash they travelled to the fortress that was the Vanden Stock Stadium in the knowledge that if Lazio failed to beat Real Madrid at the Stadio Olimpico and Leeds won in Belgium then they would be through with a game to spare.

Lose however and they would be tied on points with Anderlecht with Leeds facing the daunting tasks of a trip to the Bernabéu and a home tie with Lazio. Anderlecht would have the same task although they would be hosting Real Madrid and travelling to Rome – so it would be down to a straight shoot-out between them and Leeds. It was yet another wet and again foggy backdrop for a match between the two clubs. The Vanden Stock Stadium was a smaller arena than what Leeds had been becoming accustomed to such as the Camp Nou, San Siro, and Stadio Olimpico, with a crowd of just 28,063. It was just as atmospheric however and except for the flares that were lit, with the rain and the compact stands the setting had a feel of a very traditional English-like stadium. The ticket allocation given to travelling Leeds fans fell way short of demand as 1,200 supporters crammed into the away end.

Bowyer – unable to travel during his court case – was unavailable so Erik Bakke took his place in Leeds's only change from the home meeting, whilst Anderlecht opted for the same eleven that started at Elland Road. Anderlecht had won their last 21 consecutive home matches, including their last ten European home ties, and had a 100% home record so far in the competition having defeated PSV, Dynamo Kyiv, Manchester United, and Lazio. Unsurprisingly, the Belgians went into the game as favourites,

Dacourt's translations looked to have the desired effect from the first whistle as a fired-up United took the game to their hosts. A shot from Bakke was handled over the bar by Milojevic after some neat link-up play from Viduka and Smith. At the other end, Thomas Radzinksi came close to adding to his account of five Champions League goals when he shot just wide of the Leeds goal which a sprawling Nigel Martyn looked to have covered. But the breakthrough came on 13 minutes. Smith had made space from an Ian Harte throw-in from a seemingly harmless position just inside the Anderlecht half and Smith's first-time header opened up space behind the defence for Viduka who drove to the byline where he managed to cut back onto his stronger right foot and play a pass to Smith whose run was timed perfectly to strike first time from six yards. The two under-fire strikers linked perfectly to give Leeds the lead. It got even better for Leeds just after the half-hour mark as provider turned scorer when Viduka ended his nine-game goal drought. Some good play in midfield allowed Dom Matteo on the wide left to cross from the edge of the penalty area. His looping cross towards the back post was met by Viduka who was unable to jump over the top of the ball so instead opted for a looping header which landed over the outstretched Milojevic and into the net. Anderlecht's impenetrable home was silenced as their long winning streak at their fortress was threatened. A chance for the Belgians to get back into the game came and went when they had a penalty claim turned away after Bart Goor had tumbled inside the penalty area when under pressure from Danny Mills. Instead, the game was put further out of the Belgian's reach with perhaps the most aesthetically pleasing goal of Leeds's Champions League season so far. Some cultured play inside the midfield saw Smith, David Batty, Dacourt, and then Viduka link up neatly before Batty was able to play a perfectly timed pass in between the two Anderlecht central defenders and into the path of Smith. Milojevic came out to close down the angle for the Leeds youngster, but Smith executed an audacious deft chip over him which bounced into an empty net. Leeds had well and truly stormed the Belgian's fortress inside the first-half and the men in yellow had one foot inside the quarter-finals. David O'Leary certainly thought so, as he ran onto the pitch to celebrate the goal as Smith - arms outstretched in celebration - was mobbed by his teammates as the Leeds fans celebrated wildly in disbelief of the display their team were putting on.

Antheunis opted to make a change there and then as Aleksander Illic was handed the indignity of being replaced before half-time for Aruna Dindane. The substitution almost immediately had the desired effect as Anderlecht almost pulled one back before half-time as Koller's height allowed him to beat Rio Ferdinand to a Goor cross and his downward header flashed past Martyn's far post. Minutes later Alin Stoica blazed an effort into the stands as the Anderlecht tried to force themselves back into the game before the break but to no avail. Leeds was looking to extend their lead after the break and had protests for a penalty declined when a Harte corner was poorly dealt with and landed into the feet of Ferdinand who would have scored his first Leeds goal but for an intervention from Koller. The striker was back defending the goal line and as he turned his back on the shot, he looked to have blocked it with his arm, but referee Rune Pedersen again waved his arms instead of pointing to the spot.

At the other end, Martyn was on hand to deny Goor as he rushed quickly off his line to deny him after he was played in behind from a Radzinski header. Another chance went begging for the Romanian after an attacking free-kick evaded everyone until it found him at the far post where he could only turn his effort into the side-netting. Stoica's frustration was clear to see and reflected that of his team on the night as he booted the advertisement hoardings behind the goal. With fifteen minutes left on the clock, the Belgians did pull one back as an unmarked Koller towered above an outstretched Martyn who had come out to claim a deep free-kick but was beaten by the Czech giant. Anderlecht's fans had found their voice and demanded a chase from their team and Martyn was needed again to deny Koller - who was yet again unmarked from a Goor cutback - and struck from twelve yards – which was parried over the crossbar. Any chance of a comeback was extinguished on 81 minutes when Leeds was awarded an opportunity to well and truly put the game to bed from the penalty spot. Harte's deep free-kick was played into Viduka who was tumbled down under pressure from De Boeck climbing over his back and this time the referee did point to the penalty spot. Ian Harte assertively dispatched his spot kick and cartwheeled away in front of the travelling supporters. The goal had put the gloss on a stupendous performance away from home and those supporters were sharp to remember that their Cross-Pennine rivals had lost to them earlier in the season chanting a chorus of "Are you watching Manchester?".

Leeds United again defeated the odds in their maiden Champions League voyage, not only in becoming the first team to win at the Vanden Stock Stadium for 21 games but also in qualifying from a second group that few gave them a chance in. An equaliser from Raul Gonzalez 17 minutes from time earned Real Madrid a point in a 2-2 draw at the Stadio Olimpico and with it secured theirs and Leeds's passage into the last eight of the competition - eliminating Lazio and Anderlecht in the process. Yet again, Leeds had silenced their doubters and with two games of Group D to spare, they became the first English side to book their place in the quarter-finals.

The performances of Alan Smith and Mark Viduka were the perfect answer to their critics. O'Leary speaking to ITV post-match agreed when probed that the arrival of Robbie Keane (unavailable in Europe) had been rejuvenating for Smith as he aimed to fight for his striking berth in the team. "That's not a bad thing, but as well as that we have been able to give him a breather because of that. He played brilliantly, he went off a little bit and he had that breather and he's benefited from that as well", the Leeds boss said. Reporter Gabriel Clarke then proceeded to tell O'Leary the news of the 2-2 draw in Rome between

Lazio and Real Madrid which confirmed United's progression. O'Leary couldn't hide a proud beaming smile. "It's absolutely fantastic. I'm so proud and it's the players that have done it and I am so proud of them".

With the job done, it was now the turn of the Leeds players to throw back the negative comments thrown back at them. Antheunis's rant extended to Viduka who he had said performed poorly in the Elland Road meeting. Viduka - not content with his contribution of a goal, an assist, and his work to earn the penalty in the 4-1 win doing his talking for him – took his opportunity to tear into the Anderlecht boss. "What I will say is I hope their coach will be able to watch the quarter-final matches on his widescreen television!", he taunted.

The tensions between the two managers had peaked and O'Leary was in no forgiving mood towards his counterpart despite his triumph. At the obligatory post-match press conference, O'Leary arrived for his duties whilst Antheunis was still completing his where he was admitting that underestimating Leeds was a mistake. As the two coaches' paths crossed by the door Antheunis tried to appeal to O'Leary that "I did not say you were a bad side". O'Leary replied, "We listened to what you said and thank you. I wish you well my friend".

"I'm so proud of my players. The incentive was there to prove people wrong, and we've done just that," said O'Leary to the Guardian. "We're not a bad little team and we can only get better. I'm sure we have surprised a lot of people across Europe."

Hanging around at the Bernabéu

Vs Real Madrid (Away) and Lazio (Home)

UEFA Champions League Second Group Phase, Matchdays 5&6

Leeds was beginning to form a habit of perhaps making George Graham regret his decision to trade West Yorkshire for North London and make a mockery of the Scotsman's prophecy that Tottenham Hotspur had a bigger potential for success than Leeds United. Leeds's return to Premier League action following their decisive double-header with Anderlecht saw the Champions League quarter-finalists travel to White Hart Lane. It was a venue that Spurs had made a fortress in the league that season to date, unbeaten into late February but their inconsistent form away from home meant they were only occupying a position in mid-table. That run looked good for an extension into March when Les Ferdinand pounced on a mistake from his younger second cousin Rio to give Spurs a 33rd-minute lead. However, Ian Harte levelled the scores on the cusp of half-time and then turned provider, assisting for Lee Bowyer - scoring on his 200th appearance for The Whites - in the second half as Leeds completed the turnaround. The result put further pressure on their old boss who, despite their home form, was under fire from Chairman Sir Alan Sugar and Graham would be dismissed from his post three weeks later for a breach of his contract and would not manage a team again. The win made it 18 points from a possible 29 for Leeds since the turn of the year and that had propelled them up to sixth place. Next up was a visit from their old foes in the form of Sir Alex Ferguson's Manchester United at Elland Road in an early morning 11.30 am kick-off with Leeds knowing that a famous win would move them into the

Champions League places for the first time that season. The talk in the build-up to the game however included a Manchester United legend sitting in the Leeds dugout against his old boss and former employers with whom he had become synonymous. Brian Kidd had made 203 appearances for the Red Devils and scored on his 19th birthday in the European Cup final against Benfica at Wembley when Sir Matt Busby's side became the first English side to win the holy grail of European football in 1968. After Kidd had gone into coaching after playing retirement, he spent ten years from 1988 to 1998 as assistant to Ferguson before taking up a manager's post at Blackburn Rovers but was dismissed a year later. He joined Leeds United in the summer of 2000 originally as a youth coach with a view to eventually promoting him to first-team coach. As if by coincidence his promotion was announced in the lead-up to the 'Roses' clash at Elland Road. David O'Leary stated in his programme notes ahead of the game, "I am delighted to announce that from today Brian Kidd will become head coach of Leeds United. He's a great coach and he will be a valuable addition to our team. With him, Eddie Gray, Roy Aitken, and myself, I think we have one of the strongest and most experienced quartets you'll find anywhere and I'm confident the players will reap the benefit of that". But for Leeds fans, it was an unpopular appointment, and many questioned the need for him in the first-team set up and whether he would be stepping on the toes of club legend and current assistant Eddie Gray who had done a remarkable job nurturing the vast young talent that Leeds was now reaping the rewards from.

Lucas Radebe had stirred the imagination pre-game when stating his hope for this fixture to be the Champions League final in Milan in May. There was a lot of football to be played before that could even be considered however and attentions soon moved away from the sideshow in the dug-outs and onto the pitch in a hot-tempered affair which met boiling point shortly before the half-time whistle. Manchester United goalkeeper Fabien Barthez had kicked Ian Harte off the ball, but the incident was noticed by the officials and a penalty was awarded to Leeds. Harte got to his feet to take the penalty, and despite the incident equating to violent conduct Barthez escaped with only a yellow card. To rub salt into Leeds's wounds the Frenchman saved Harte's spot kick. The home team's frustrations grew further in the second half when Luke Chadwick gave the visitors the lead with just a quarter of the game remaining. Leeds had performed well however and got a deserved equaliser from a header by Mark Viduka with six minutes left on the clock. With the atmosphere now at fever pitch and the Leeds players smelling blood there was still time for a winner and Leeds thought they had one in the final minute of the game. Manchester United defender Wes Brown converted a Bowyer cross into his own goal to send Elland Road delirious only for the assistant referee to rule the goal out incorrectly for offside. The two points that were denied by Leeds would later have severe consequences – yet to be known.

***

Peter Ridsdale urged for some reflection ahead of the two games against Manchester United and Real Madrid. Before we start to consider our chances against these two Goliaths of football, we should first of all remember that just a few years ago we would have dreamt of being involved in back-to-back matches like these". However, the mindset at Leeds had now changed and where there was once an inferiority complex - particularly with Manchester United - there was now an air of confidence that their team could compete with the best. Despite that, when the fixtures were laid out for Group D of the second phase of the Champions League, there would have been apprehension at the thought of Leeds needing results against Real Madrid and Lazio in their final two games. But now the club had the luxury of travelling to the most famous club in World football knowing that their fate had already been sealed ahead of their game with fellow qualifiers Real Madrid.

With the draw having been made back in November, Leeds fans had almost four months to save up for a once-in-a-lifetime trip to see their team play at the Santiago Bernabéu Stadium. Leeds was initially allocated 3,000 tickets which were snapped up instantly but many thousands more made the trip regardless as a Yorkshire invasion set upon the Spanish capital. Those that did make the trip from England to Madrid were made to walk through specially disinfected carpets at Madrid airport designed to prevent the spread of the foot and mouth disease that was discovered at an Essex abattoir on 19th February 2001. There were also subsequently denied reports that Real Madrid had asked the Leeds players to wear new boots. Upon arrival in Madrid though, it wasn't just the Leeds fans that were caught up in the novelty and excitement of the occasion. The young Leeds squad was soaking up the experience as Dom Matteo explains in his autobiography *In My Defence,* "Our training session on the eve of the match (on the Bernabéu pitch) lasted for about three hours because no one wanted to leave. In the end, the groundsman had to come on the field to kick us off. The only Englishman not happy with our extended session was Steve McManaman, who had come down for a chat but had to hang around for ages before I was free". The next night, the game being effectively a dead rubber failed to inspire the 'Madridista' support to brave the heavy showers Spain was experiencing and there were large pockets of empty seats around the stadium. An attendance of 39,460 meant the arena was less than half full. The travelling Leeds hoards without tickets eager not to miss out were purchasing tickets in the home sections of the stadium before Real granted United fans an extra 5000 tickets.

The unofficial total of 8,000 Leeds fans made it the club's biggest-ever support on the continent for a non-final tie.

Whilst both teams already had their passage into the quarter-finals assured there was the financial incentive for their clubs in the form of UEFA's £300,000 win bonus in the Champions League but professional pride was on show in abundance once the game started. Real were looking almost unbeatable and had lost only one of their last 18 games in all competitions since losing the Intercontinental Cup final to Argentine side Boca Juniors in November 2000. Real respected Leeds and the competition with their strongest available line-up too missing only the suspended Ivan Helgura and Roberto Carlos who was away on international duty with Brazil. Leeds was also missing Danny Mills through suspension but called upon Harry Kewell for his first start since Boxing Day and Lucas Radebe made the line-up despite missing the team's extended training session the night before managing a knee injury.

Real Madrid had never lost at home to an English side in the seven previous European ties, but that record was under threat only six minutes into the game. Mark Viduka picked up a clearance from Radebe inside the Leeds half and managed to turn and run away from the Madrid midfield before playing a neat through ball into the path of Alan Smith who had the beating of the surrounding defence. Goalkeeper Cesar Sanchez Dominguez came out to close Smith down, but he couldn't prevent the Leeds man from slotting the ball past him and into the net. The assistant referee's flag stayed down despite a questionable offside offense and 8000 Leeds fans were in raptures. Those fans were still celebrating however when Real immediately levelled the scores controversially.

A foul committed on Santiago Solari by Erik Bakke presented Luis Figo with a free-kick in an ideal crossing position just outside the penalty area. The Portuguese's kick was met and converted by Raul. However, he did well to deceive the referee as he turned the ball in using his outstretched right arm. Nigel Martyn and Radebe were quick to protest on the pitch and O'Leary and the Leeds bench also made their protestations to Polish referee Ryszard Wojcik but the goal was given. Not deterred from the injustice, Smith had a golden opportunity to double his tally on the night and put Leeds back in front when completely unmarked from six yards out, he could only head Kewell's cross from the left side into the ground and towards Cesar. Instead, it was the home side that went into the half-time break with the lead. On 41 minutes Figo drove down the right flank arching a cross around Batty from the edge of the penalty area. Fernando Morientes was lurking as Martyn came out to thwart him, but the ball took a very fortunate bobble for the Portuguese and found its way into the back of the net. Leeds had battled well but had found themselves behind courtesy of a handball and what can be best described as a fluke. Ten minutes into the second-half Kewell had forced Geremi into conceding a corner and an inviting cross from Ian Harte towards the centre of the six-yard box was met by Viduka who capitalised on some poor marking from Madrid and headed powerfully through the legs of Cesar and Leeds were back level. A small pocket of Leeds fans in the home end had the perfect view behind Cesar's goal. At the other end, a fantastic last-ditch tackle was needed by Radebe to deny the pantomime villain of the night – Raul - as he was about to pull the trigger – taking ball and man - and the referee rightly ignored Madrid's penalty claims. But Real were eventually back in front for the second time on the night. Figo collected a short corner and played in a dangerous cross into Raul who this time converted legitimately with his head jumping above Matteo. Matters were made worse for Leeds when Radebe had to leave the pitch on the stretcher after aggravating his knee injury and was replaced by Gary Kelly. Leeds was still in the contest however and Kewell's pace was causing Geremi problems all evening. The Leeds winger would go home with the keepsake of his opponent's shirt- and he beat the Cameroonian's two-footed lunge just inside the Madrid half and was able to commit their defence before playing a ball into Smith who worked it out wide to an unmarked Viduka. The Aussie's powerful shot clipped the woodwork where crossbar meets post and minutes later, Smith was again played in by Viduka who pierced a pass through Madrid's back line but Smith was denied a repeat of his earlier goal and with that Leeds's chances had gone. There was little jeopardy in defeat and Leeds could be happy with their performance in an entertaining contest but that did little to extinguish their annoyance at the injustice of Raul handling the ball into the goal to draw the teams' level just after Leeds had taken the lead. O'Leary was frustrated but philosophical post-match speaking to Don Warters and explained, "I was proud of my players. We didn't deserve to lose. You just cannot legislate for goals such as Real's first and second. I felt we were always a threat to Real and this performance was not a one-off either. We have played some tremendous football in Europe all season". Leeds gained further praise from Englishman in Madrid McManaman who tipped this young Leeds team to become one of the best teams in Europe in the coming years. "It has been no surprise at all to see the progress they have made over the past couple of years as the kids have got that bit older and wiser. You wonder what kind of team they might be in another two or three-years' time", he praised. Referee Wojcik visited an angry Leeds dressing room after the game to apologise and admit to his mistake in awarding Raul's first goal after watching a television replay. He didn't get any sympathy from Oliver Dacourt, however.

"The players have to prove they are good enough to get through each stage and maybe it should be the same with referees. He was very bad for us. He apologised but that does not really count as we lost the game. To play so well and lose because of one decision like that is very difficult to take", the Frenchman stated. UEFA had initially handed Raul a one-match ban and a fine of €8000 for the deceiving offense but a UEFA appeals committee eventually overturned the penalty as the referee had been unable to make a factual decision. Raul didn't escape all punishment as he was pillorised by sections of the Spanish media for disgracing the good name of Spanish football, yet he still received a reward a few days later for being voted Spain's most popular sportsman. The trophy he received was ironically a sculpture of a hand holding a heart!

***

Leeds's fourth-round exit from the FA Cup again had its advantages as O'Leary's side had a weekend's break from domestic action before they welcomed Lazio to Elland Road to polish off their Group D campaign. Lazio had disappointed in this group and were sitting on just four points from their five games and elimination was already confirmed. It was proving to be a difficult season for the star-studded Italian champions who had struggled to build on their first Scudetto success since 1974 (and would eventually surrender their title to city rivals Roma) and suffered an early elimination from the Coppa Italia at the hands of Sampdoria. Since the two club's last meeting over three months before manager Sven Goran Eriksson had departed Rome earlier than scheduled to take up his new role as England manager. The Swede had got off to an ideal start as manager of the Three Lions with a 3-0 win over Spain in a friendly at Villa Park with a team that included Leeds men Nigel Martyn and Rio

Ferdinand. Replacing Eriksson in the Lazio hot seat was legendary former Italian goalkeeper Dino Zoff. Zoff had previously managed the club over two spells in the mid 1990's and less than a year prior was a minute away from leading Italy to Euro 2000 glory. Results had picked up since he took the reigns over the new year. He immediately led Lazio to four wins on the bounce and they were enjoying a ten-game unbeaten run before arriving in England on the back of a 3-0 away defeat to Bologna.

For what was essentially another dead rubber, unlike in Madrid, both teams did ring the changes for this clash. Leeds had their continued European interest in mind as they decided against risking Alan Smith and Erik Bakke getting a booking which would see them suspended for the quarter-finals. O'Leary also had one eye on his team's resurrected European push for next season. Ahead of this game and the following weekend's trip to The Valley to face Charlton Athletic, O'Leary stated "We want to sign off from Group D in style but if you made me choose one win out of two, I'd rather we beat Charlton on Saturday. We've attained our goal in the UEFA Champions League by qualifying from this group, but we've still got a lot of work to do in the league". Therefore, he opted to give the night off to Ferdinand, David Batty, and Olivier Dacourt whilst giving Paul Robinson another chance in goal. Gary Kelly took the captain's armband; Jacob Burns made a rare start as did Jason Wilcox but most interestingly there was a first Leeds start in over three years for reserve team player Alan Maybury. Danny Mills and Dom Matteo made an unusual centre-back pairing. O'Leary later admitted in *Leeds United on Trial* that there was some disquiet that so many changes could see Leeds on the end of heavy beating, but the Irishman was confident that his pragmatic approach wouldn't result in that. Nevertheless, Lazio themselves had an eye on an important Serie A game with Juventus coming up the following weekend and they too experimented with their line-up which was without Angelo Peruzzi, Alessandro Nesta, Guiseppe Favalli, Guerino Gottardi, Diego Simeone, Juan Sebastian Veron and Flippo Inzaghi.

Despite the cast list being different and the plot less intriguing as first advertised, what transpired was an enjoyable free-flowing evening of football - and as ever when Leeds United was involved – not without controversy. The visitors drew first blood on 21 minutes through former Middlesbrough striker Fabrizio Ravanelli. Leeds had been penned back towards their own goal and a cross from Pavel Nedved was directed in-between Mills and Kelly towards Ravanelli and the silver-haired striker headed past Robinson from six yards out. The Roman's lead had only lasted seven minutes, however. Kewell had attempted a cross into the Lazio penalty but was blocked before rebounding back to him where he played in Bowyer - who from a ludicrously tight angle and whilst facing away from goal – swivelled and pulled off a deft lofted shot that had goalkeeper Luca Marchegiani beaten. The goal put Bowyer level at the top of the competition's Golden Boot race. Football was again a welcome respite from the realities of the ongoing court case for Bowyer which was high profile in the public's interest with details relayed through the tabloids each day. One such story told of how Bowyer was asked to get changed at court by his brief but mentioned that he couldn't at that moment as he wasn't wearing any underwear. A chant for Bowyer from the Leeds faithful went "He's here, he's there, he's every-F***ing-where Lee Bowyer, Lee Bowyer". It was after this goal that the lyrics were playfully changed to, "he wears no underwear". This song was still ringing around Elland Road when parity in the scoreline was again removed. Straight from the restart a long-lofted ball played into the Leeds penalty area caused panic and Matteo pulled back the run of Ravanelli. A penalty was awarded which was despatched high into the right side of the net by set-piece specialist Sinisa Mihajlovic. As the pendulum swung yet again in this game Leeds again drew level just before half-time. Maybury had won a corner out of Fernando Couto and Kewell's corner deep towards the back-post was volleyed in first-time hard and low from the left foot of Wilcox two minutes before an entertaining first-half was drawn to a close. Leeds made a strong start to the second half and soon led for the first time on the night. After Kewell had drawn a foul on the wide right from Mihajlovic, Ian Harte's free-kick into the penalty area was headed goal-bound by Mark Viduka. That was Viduka's last involvement before being withdrawn and replaced by Tony Hackworth who was granted a rare appearance. Hackworth almost had an immediate impact when his cross from the wide left was met by Kewell, but his header was saved by Marchegiani to prevent Leeds from going further ahead. At the other end, Mihajlovic forced Robinson into a good save with a free-kick which took a deflection, but the Yugoslav would eventually have the last laugh. Marcelo Salas came close to equalising for Lazio when he struck a post almost punishing a mistake from Jacob Burns who attempted a flick under pressure just outside his own penalty area which brought him an ear bashing from his manager on the touchline. Despite the game being essentially a formality of fulfilling the fixture list, the game was played as if qualification was still up for grabs, even if the noise from the crowd suggested a lack of intensity. As the game was drawing to a close and with yet another impressive Leeds scalp within sight, Alan Maybury was lucky not to suffer a serious injury when Pavel Nedved planted his studs high into his knee. The Czech suffered no further (immediate) punishment whilst Maybury was forced out of action and replaced by Batty, yet amazingly the referee - Konrad Plautz of Austria - awarded Lazio with a free-kick close to Robinson's goal in stoppage time. Milajovic this time got the better of the young Leeds goalkeeper, steering a delightful free-kick over the Leeds defensive wall and into the top corner giving Robinson no chance and with it ensuring the points were shared. It was the second consecutive European game in which Leeds had felt aggrieved at a disciplinary injustice but unlike with Raul before, future Ballon D'or winner Nedved was retrospectively banned for three games and this time UEFA stuck to their guns. Nedved was granted access to the home dressing room to personally apologise to Maybury after the game. On the pitch, the Lazio players celebrated securing a draw with the last kick of the game but on the bigger picture it was the Italians who were fancied to progress from Group D along with Real Madrid when the draw was made back in November, yet it was Leeds who were looking ahead to the upcoming quarter-final draw. The draw also meant Leeds kept intact their proud record of never losing to Italian opposition at Elland Road.

Elsewhere Real Madrid also lost at Anderlecht further showing how impressive and key Leeds's earlier win in Belgium was. Joining Leeds in the last eight were compatriots Manchester United and Arsenal who squeezed through despite losing their final group match away at Bayern Munich but edged out Lyon on the head-to-head rule after the French team spurned their chance of progression, only managing a draw with Spartak Moscow. The rest of the cast list was made up of Bayern Munich, Galatasaray, and Spanish trio Valencia, Real Madrid, and Deportivo La Coruna. Esteemed company indeed but after surviving and thriving in not one but two 'Groups of Death' the attitude of Leeds United was 'bring it on'.

3-0 To the Weakest Team

Vs Deportivo La Coruna

UEFA Champions League Quarter-Final

"I suppose you have to give them some credit for putting out Barcelona and qualifying alongside Madrid, but we were very pleased when we heard Leeds would be our next opponents. They are the weakest team in the competition and when you compare them to the other sides, we've got the easiest draw." These were the words of Deportivo La Coruna midfielder Victor Sanchez Del Amo following the quarter-final draw which drew two of the Champions League newcomers, yet two of the most exciting teams remaining in the competition together. There may have been some credibility to Victor's statement at the time. Leeds United may have been a more favourable prospect than others in the draw that Deportivo could have been paired with such as Manchester United, Arsenal, and Bayern Munich. Also, in hindsight, nearly a quarter of a century on where Deportivo now plies their trade in the third tier of Spanish football you could be forgiven for Leeds counting their blessings that they had drawn a club without the pedigree of Bayern Munich, Valencia, either of their English neighbours, Arsenal and Manchester United or a nightmare reunion with Galatasaray - all of which was possible. But this Deportivo team were the current champions of Spain and were developing into one of the most revered sides in Europe who themselves were taking the Champions League by storm on their first foray in the competition. The Spaniards had won both of their groups eliminating illustrious names such as Juventus, Paris Saint Germain, and AC Milan along the way. A run of five wins, five draws and only two defeats slightly bettered Leeds's record of five wins, four draws, and three defeats in the competition. Despite football in Spain originating in the northern cities such as Bilbao, San Sebastian, and La Coruna, as a footballing force, Deportivo had a largely unrecognisable history before the 1990s. Since winning promotion to La Liga in 1991 they had wrestled their way into competition with Spanish football's illustrious hierarchy and won the Copa Del Rey (Spain's equivalent of the FA Cup) in 1995. In the mid-nineties, they were regulars in the higher echelons of the league finishing in third place in 1993 and 1997 and in-between becoming runners-up in 1994 and in 1995. Their eventual league title triumph in 1999/2000 - in which they finished five points ahead of runners-up Barcelona – would have done a lot to remedy the painful wounds that existed from the final day of the **1993-94** season. Needing to beat Valencia to win a maiden league title, they were tied at 0-0 when they were awarded a penalty in the final minute. Miroslav Djukić had the opportunity to seal glory but his spot kick was missed and Barcelona pipped Deportivo to the title courtesy of a better head-to-head goal average. For the 2000-01 vintage, Deportivo managed by Javier Irueta was a team full of flair and skill but lacking any real household names. Striker Roy Makaay was the most renowned player in their ranks whilst their top goal scorer in the Champions League was Walter Pandiani with five goals before the quarter-finals and Brazilian attacking midfielder Djalminha was interesting many potential suitors across Europe with his fine displays. Also in their ranks was future a World Cup winner in the form of left-back Joan Capdevila (Span 2010) and they also had midfielder Emerson who in a parallel universe would have been Brazil's 2002 World Cup-winning captain had he not sustained a dislocated shoulder in training on the eve of the tournament.

So, the pair-up of this exciting Deportivo team and a Leeds team completely resurgent domestically now as well as in Europe was a mouthwatering proposition. Leeds continued their surge up the Premier League before the Quarter-final 1st leg scheduled to take place at Elland Road with back-to-back away wins over Charlton Athletic and Sunderland. At The Valley, Charlton, Mark Viduka gave Leeds the lead within seconds of the kick-off before future Leeds man Radostin Kishishev equalised for 'The Addicks'. The second half started just as blisteringly for Leeds though as Alan Smith too scored within one minute of the whistle and Leeds were 2-1 victors. A week later, on the day the football world mourned the death of former Leeds and Arsenal player David Rocastle at the tragically young age of 33, Leeds saw off the challenge of Sunderland at the Stadium of Light. Smith and Viduka were again the match winners but after Smith had given Leeds a first-half lead he later received a straight red card twenty minutes from time making for a nervy ending before Viduka made sure of the points in the final minute with his 20th goal of the season.

As attentions turned to, arguably, Elland Road's biggest occasion for 26 years, the words from Victor after the draw resurfaced as the Leeds squad took exception to yet again being underestimated and shown a lack of respect for their achievements so far. Erik Bakke was the first to bite back with the Norwegian international telling the press, "Victor can say what he likes. We know we are not the weakest team left in the competition. He is only saying what Lazio, AC Milan, and all those teams said about us, and look where they are now - out of the tournament. I have seen Deportivo on television a couple of times, and they are very strong, but we have beaten better teams than them earlier in the competition. They won the Spanish League last season, but we know we can beat them over two legs, that's for sure", the Norwegian quipped. Victor's comments were also a red rag to a bull to Rio Ferdinand. "We will do our talking on the pitch. If people say things like that it makes us all the more determined to prove them wrong and the same applies to what this guy has said. We've had it a lot in this competition – especially against Anderlecht – and it brings the boys a lot closer together", he said. David O'Leary was more diplomatic and humbler in his approach to the game respecting the level of the opposition that lay ahead of his team. "There are eight teams left and we would probably be the eighth seed in that group, so Deportivo will be delighted with the draw. The other seven would have loved to have got us" the Leeds gaffer stated in his programme notes on matchday. Perhaps concerned that Victor had performed O'Leary's pre-match **team talk for him, the Deportivo manager, like his Anderlecht counterpart Aime Antheunis before** him, tried to throw water on the fire by stating that he believed Leeds are as good as Manchester United, but the damage was already done in the eyes of the Leeds camp.

There were reports in the build-up to the game that Deportivo could have been thrown out of the competition leaving Leeds with a free route to the semi-finals, due to allegations of false passports being held by some of their players. Jacques Songo'o, Aldo Pedro Duscher, Helder, and Emerson were all namechecked in the allegations. UEFA launched an investigation, but no wrongdoing was found.

In team news ahead of the game Alan Smith faced a race to be fit after picking up a calf injury before his dismissal at Sunderland. Smith would make the starting line-up, but skipper Lucas Radebe was not so fortunate. The South African was risked despite nursing a knee injury for the trip to the Stadium of Light but that backfired as he sustained a season-ending injury to his other knee. Rio Ferdinand who had adjusted remarkably quickly to Elland Road life was given the armband from O'Leary at the age of just 22 and would keep it on his arm for the rest of his Leeds career. Despite Radebe's injury, O'Leary was able to name perhaps his strongest and most favourable line-up yet in the Champions League; Martyn, Mills, Harte, Ferdinand, Matteo, Bowyer, Dacourt, Batty, Kewell, Smith, Viduka. The quarter-finals got underway the night before on Tuesday 3rd April, with shocks. Galatasaray defeated Real Madrid 3-2 and Bayern Munich secured a late 1-0 win against Manchester United at Old Trafford. Simultaneously to Leeds United V Deportivo La Coruna, 192 miles away at Highbury, Arsenal took a 2-1 advantage over Valencia. But it was the clash at Elland Road that sparked the football purists' imagination with two unfamiliar names for this stage that had a habit of upsetting the odds and pleasing neutrals with their fearless football over the past couple of seasons jousting for an improbable semi-final place and the tie was duly selected for the primetime viewing on ITV. In his wonderful way with words, commentator for the evening Peter Drury beautifully articulated the narrative of the game as the two teams lined up for the obligatory anthem.

"Two queues of men that began the season as Champions League debutants and just took to it. Real Madrid - the best team in Europe but illogically, the Spaniards will tell you this is the best team in Spain. And only Real Madrid have beaten Leeds in their last dozen games. This is the form team in England".

Amid a raucous atmosphere, the first chance of the game arrived for Harry Kewell after the Australian came close to completing an outrageous piece of skill with a goal. After collecting the ball from Alan Smith on the wide left, a first-time chip had got him past Pedro Duscher and a second chip saw him evade Manuel Pablo before unleashing an effort from an acute angle near the touchline which blazed just over the bar. The audacious skill from Kewell raised the decibel levels inside Elland Road, not that they needed raising. Leeds had a reward for their bright start on 27 minutes. A through ball from Dacourt pierced the Deportivo midfield and played in Smith at the edge of the penalty area where he was tumbled down by Cesar Villar. Ian Harte and Dacourt stood over the free-kick but there was only ever going to be one man to take it. From 20 yards in front of the Kop, Harte's kick was blasted around a six-man Spanish wall and past goalkeeper Francisco Molina before he could even see it coming. "Bullseye", screamed Drury. Harte reminisced over this strike speaking to *FourFourTwo* magazine in 2024. "I hit the ball as hard as I could, and it flew in off the crossbar. Whenever I took free-kicks, I imagined lines on a motorway and tried to strike the ball within those. I always used to visualise where I wanted to place my free-kicks, which I would combine with my technique", he said. Leeds, roared on by the crowd and encouraged by their blinding start to the game, were playing as if they had an extra man than their opponents. They should have doubled their lead when Kewell played in an inviting first-time cross from the wide-left which floated through to a diving Smith whose header off target really should have found the back of the net.

The Leeds players left the pitch at the end of the first half to the sound of a deafening ovation, and they started the second half just as they finished the first. Smith desperate to atone for his earlier miss drew a save from Molina with a right-footed shot from the edge of the area forcing a corner. The resulting corner was initially cleared by Djalma Dias but as seemed to be the case every time Deportivo tried to escape their goal they were pushed back. Dacourt collected the ball just inside the final third and played in Harte whose cross was better than his initial corner and was headed home by Smith who squeezed in-between Nourredine Naybet and Enrique Romero to eventually get the goal he had been threatening all night – his downwards header from six yards finally beating Molina.

On 66 minutes, Leeds United were in dreamland. After Harte and Kewell had attempted a short corner only for it to be blocked for another one, Harte opted the second time round to play a cross directly into the penalty area. Molina came off his line to claim the cross from the front post but substitute Juan Carlos Valeron headed the ball over him as he did so. The ball was directed fortuitously into the path of Ferdinand towards the back post who headed into a goal unguarded by the goalkeeper and past the three defenders on the goal line. It was new skipper Rio's first goal in the white of Leeds and his superlative performance earned him an incredibly rare 10/10 rating in the Yorkshire Evening Post. A popular early evening television show at the time was *The Weakest Link* featuring arrogant host Anne Robinson, where she would dismiss eliminated contestants with the jibe, "You are the weakest link, goodbye" supplemented with a petulant wink. Leeds fans, remembering Deportivo midfielder Victor (who was an unused substitute in the game) using a similar adjective to describe their team came out with a rousing ditty of "3-0 to the weakest team". For them, with Leeds having one foot in the semi-finals already, they were dreaming of dismissing their visitors with Robinson's famous catchphrase.

Despite Leeds looking like they could wrap up the tie here and now, O'Leary had warned his troops pre-match that it was critical his team did not concede an away goal for Deportivo to take back to La Coruna. As the game was drawing to a close, Nigel Maryn who had a quiet night up to this point was needed to make a save from Uruguayan Pandiani in the final minute and again from the resulting corner to punch the ball away at the near post. Despite the Spaniards proving no threat all evening, in added time Leeds were defending their goal as if the tie revolved around it as they aimed to prevent Deportivo from salvaging a valuable away goal against a backdrop of deafening whistles every time someone in blue and white stripes were touching the ball and pleading for the referee to blow for full-time. The final whistle was greeted with glee from the supporters and Viduka raised both arms aloft and Leeds could be forgiven for thinking it was job done. "Leeds on top of their game, on top of the world, and looking at a European Cup semi-final", summarised Drury on commentary.

Watching the game back two decades on for *The Athletic*, journalist Phil Hay asked Nigel Martyn - a mainstay in the Leeds side for six years – if that Leeds side ever played better to which he admitted that they hadn't. "No not in one game. Spells here and there, maybe, but never 90 minutes like that. It's controlled and it's overwhelming. You're looking at a team at its peak", Martyn replied.

O'Leary was cautious with his post-match comments despite admitting it was his best result yet as Leeds boss. "It is only half-time. We still have to face them in the second leg, and I have seen these advantages wiped out before. We now have to go and finish the job". Olivier Dacourt who seemed to revel in a war of words after translating comments made by Anderlecht to his teammates earlier in the competition was quick to stick the boot into his Spanish rivals. "Their manager said we were the worst team in the competition, but I don't think we're so bad. When we played Anderlecht, we showed that people shouldn't speak before a game. Another manager did and once again we have proved him wrong. I must say thank you very much to the manager of La Coruna for saying things like he did, and we are very happy!", the French midfield general quipped.

***

In between the two legs, Leeds continued their assault on the Premier League's European qualification places with another six points stretching their winning run to four in the league. A disciplined 2-0 victory over Southampton was secured at Elland Road three days after the Deportivo win. Harry Kewell gave Leeds a first half lead and Robbie Keane wrapped up the victory with an impressive, lobbed finish in the second half. Next up came a critical encounter with Liverpool at Anfield in the race for the third and last realistic Champions League qualification place for the next season. Leeds looked to be making minimal fuss off the occasion when Rio Ferdinand doubled his Leeds goal tally as early as the fourth minute and Lee Bowyer also scored as United raced into a 2-0 half-time lead. Steven Gerrard halved the arrears for the home side shortly after the break but then damaged his team's chances of a comeback following a straight red card for a reckless challenge on David Batty. Leeds held out to gain an invaluable three points as they opened up a six-point gap over Liverpool albeit having played two games more.

***

More impactfully, however, was the ever-growing exposure on affairs of the pitch - specifically at Hull Crown Court. In between the victories over Southampton and Liverpool came the seismic news that the high-profile court case involving several Leeds United players had been halted suddenly by Justice David Poole on Monday 9th April. The decision came as a result of an exclusive article published in the Sunday Mirror the day before involving the victim Sarfraz Najeib's father, Muhammed. The interview was published by the tabloid under the headline "I wish I had fled Britain when I was battered by racists". In the interview, Muhammad referred to a racist attack on himself and suggested that the assault on his son was also racially motivated. The article was seen by several members of the jury and subsequently led to Justice Poole abandoning the case and dismissing the jury. He was quoted as saying such allegations made in a "mass circulation newspaper published yesterday within three days of the jury's retirement... carries with it a substantial risk of prejudice" and therefore would make any verdict unsafe. For Leeds United and its players, it was a frustrating experience as the dark cloud that had been hanging over Elland Road was diluting the enjoyment of one of the club's most successful and exciting periods on the pitch in recent times. On a more serious note, the course of potential justice was delayed, and a highly sensitive court case played out in the public eye which has cost the taxpayer in the region of £10 million to date was up in smoke. After hearing eight weeks of evidence Woodgate, Paul Clifford, Neale Caveney, and Michael Duberry, were cleared of conspiracy to pervert the course of justice by the jury, however, after 21 hours of deliberation, the jury was yet to return a verdict on the affray charges when they were dismissed. A retrial was subsequently set for October 8th, 2001, meaning that the soap opera would plague Leeds United into a third season when the legal proceedings re-commenced.

***

However, in footballing matters, Leeds had their domestic house in order with their revived Premier League form being their best for over a year since they topped the division at the turn of the millennium. Therefore, an expectant Leeds team travelled to Spain for the third time that season for the second leg. Whilst many Leeds supporters wanted to join the occasion, Deportivo initially, only handed Leeds fans 850 tickets for the game at the Riazor Stadium on 17th April. A Leeds United delegation led by operations director David Spencer flew out to Spain to negotiate a bigger allocation for the travelling Whites. "Under

UEFA rules, we are entitled to receive a minimum of five percent of their capacity and that alone should give us 1,700. Deportivo will be made well aware of how seriously we view this situation. I am sure that, in the end, demand will exceed supply, but United supporters are assured that we are doing our best", Spencer stated. The next day Leeds was granted their minimum allocation of 1,700 tickets. With many more than that number wishing to travel, Spanish authorities urged Leeds fans without tickets not to travel as they would not be allowed in the home areas. There would be no repeat of the Madrid invasion. Unfortunately, for Leeds fans with tickets in the away enclosure, over 300 away fans who brought tickets for the Deportivo sections of the stadium were ushered by police to the already full away end making for a cramped, unpleasant, and unsafe experience for all.

Coruna is somewhat of an outpost on the north-west coast of Spain in the Galicia region known as the wettest place in the usually sun-soaked country. Deportivo's Estadio Riazor, benefited highly from being selected as one of the seventeen venues used for the 1982 World Cup, hosting three games, with renovations seeing its capacity rise to 34,889. Characteristically, it possesses a 100m athletic track running along one side of the stadium. However, the other stands, painted in Deportivo's blue and white stripes are tightly compact such is the way with most Spanish stadia, and are built virtually on one of the city's many beaches.

As the game approached, Leeds's 3-0 lead seemed as if it was decreasing in value over time as a realisation crept in that it wasn't quite game over just yet. Just over a month earlier in the competition, Deportivo had pulled off one of the most remarkable comebacks in Champions League history. In their penultimate second-phase Group B game they were trailing Paris Saint

Germain 3-0 in the 55th minute and their place in the competition was looking perilous. That was before two strikes from Walter Pandiani either side of a goal from Diego Tristán levelled the scores before Pandiani completed his hat-trick with a sensational winner six minutes from time. They needed just 31 minutes to complete the turnaround over PSG. They had 90 minutes to inflict the same on Leeds United. Not only that but the Riazor had become somewhat of a fortress for them just as the Vanden Stock stadium had been for Anderlecht before Leeds flexed their muscles in Brussels. AC Milan was the only travelling victors in the last 31 games they had played on home soil dating back to 5th January 2000. No wonder then that confidence was high amongst the Spanish supporters despite the mountainous task ahead of their side. Scorelines of 4-0 and 5-0 were boastfully predicted by their fans and hurled the way of Leeds fans pre-game.

David O'Leary was more cautious in his comments before the game. Speaking to Don Warters he said, "You only have to look at their home record to realise that the job we started in the first leg is far from finished. My players are hungry to get through and with a bit of luck, they will do so. They have given themselves a good chance for this great adventure to continue but they will certainly not be complacent. We have got this far after starting in the qualifying round and I think that takes some pressure off us because nobody is going to accuse us of underachieving".

But as if lessons hadn't been learned over giving this Leeds United team added ammunition, Deportivo boss Javier Irueta's summary of the Elland Road clash completely ignored United's dominance and merit in victory. "They scored their first goal at a crucial time and if you sum up the goals one was from a free-kick and the other two from corners. If you take those situations out of it we kind of matched them."

In line with the home fans' optimism that they could still progress from the tie, a blue and white ticker tape reception greeted the two teams as they emerged from the tunnel. Alan Smith, David Batty, Olivier Dacourt and Dominic Matteo were all walking a disciplinary tightrope, only one yellow card from a suspension for the semi-final should Leeds leave the Riazor stadium unscathed, but the quartet started the game regardless as O'Leary went unchanged from the side that won the first-leg. Perhaps one piece of good news regarding the halting of the trial was that Lee Bowyer was now eligible to play on the continent for the first time since the trip to Rome and the win over Lazio back in December.

Predictably, it was a fast start from the hosts – penning Leeds back early doors mirroring the narrative of the first leg. Pandiani was the first to come close but his effort inside the box was blocked by Matteo.

O'Leary later mentioned in *Leeds United on Trial* that on the day he sensed for the first time some apprehension from his players once they took to the pitch. "They seemed to be handicapped by the awareness that they were so near to the semi-final and had that three-goal insurance policy". That apprehension coupled with Deportivo's early relentless pressure only took nine minutes to take heed as the hosts won a penalty after Kewell brought down Victor Sanchez as he was about to head home at the back post. Nigel Martyn took one step to his right but was then rooted to his spot as he was outwitted by Djalminha who slotted in his penalty to pull one back for Deportivo. Leeds now knew that they would have a long, long night ahead of them to protect their lead from the first leg. The deficit was almost immediately gnawed at further as a left-footed cross from captain Francisco Perez ('Fran') looked instead to be sailing goalwards only to strike the far post. Leeds then avoided conceding a second penalty when Fran was deemed to have dived from a challenge from Dacourt. Matteo was again on hand to block a close-range effort, this time from Roy Mackaay before Martyn was on hand to deny Pandiani on two different occasions before the half-time break.

Shortly before half-time, Leeds did have the chance of that solitary away goal that would surely put the tie to bed. Smith intercepted a headed back pass from a defender towards goalkeeper Molina whom Smith rounded but the Leeds striker took his angle too wide and could only find the side-netting of an open goal. Leeds had reached the halfway stage of the game with two of their three-goal lead intact despite a relentless Spanish onslaught on their goal. However, they surely wouldn't be able to sustain much more of the punishment being dished out to them. The Deportivo pressure resumed immediately along with the second-half and a last-ditch header from Ian Harte at the back post was needed to deny Victor. Martyn also pulled off a brilliant one-handed save onto the crossbar to deny a long-range effort from Enrique Romero. Leeds managed a rare foray into the Deportivo half, but a chance fell to the wrong man from an attacking perspective in the form of Dacourt whose self-created one-on-one effort was saved by Molina. That chance was a rare period of respite for the Leeds defence before La Coruna continued their efforts at a comeback, but numerous efforts failed to trouble Martyn in the Leeds goal. Makaay came mightily close as he struck the crossbar with a headed effort after getting in between Ferdinand and Mills.

But with seventeen minutes remaining, Deportivo had finally gnawed Leeds's lead down to just one goal. Diego Tristan who had been brought on just after the hour mark converted at Martyn's near post from two yards out as the Riazor Stadium shook to its foundations as the home fans sensed another famous comeback and Leeds had a nail-biting ending to see out. Mark Viduka almost eased those nerves soon after, however, but his shot was saved by Molina. Leeds had expected the Alamo from Deportivo in the final stages but as the clock ticked towards 90 minutes the pressure from Deportivo relented in intensity. The only chance Leeds had to deal with was met by Martyn as he punched away a cross from the captain just as Tristan was lurking. Eddie Gray gave his thoughts on the limp end from the hosts and the reasons for the Leeds team playing within themselves. "Strange as it might seem when looking at our collapse in the second leg, I don't think having a three-goal lead helped us. Deportivo got the start they wanted with their penalty goal after nine minutes and, with nothing to lose, threw everything at us. The thought of the previously unthinkable happening – losing the lead – got to us. But when Deportivo made it 2-0 near the end, they started panicking as well. Instead of continuing to probe for clear-cut openings they were shooting from virtually anywhere. We regained our composure whereas they lost theirs", he reflected in his autobiography released later that year. It had been a hellish night, and a much more uncomfortable night than their 3-0 lead going into the game would have suggested. A relieved Leeds team exchanged high-fives and hugs as the two managers shared a respectful embrace at the end of a compelling two-legged encounter between two of the most enjoyable up-and-coming sides in Europe. Leeds United were through to their first European Cup semi-final since they faced off with Johan Cruyff's Barcelona 26 years before. Yet, the overwhelming feeling amongst the Leeds team was of relief rather than solely pride and jubilation after a torrid evening where they had almost spurned what had seemed an unassailable lead a fortnight earlier. Alan Smith revealed a subdued atmosphere in the Leeds dressing room post-game. "There are a lot of other teams who would love to be where we are, so we have to be happy that we have got this far. Having said that, it was a relief when the referee blew, and we were through 3-2 on aggregate. If you had been in the dressing room after the game, you would not think we had just got through to the semi-finals. We were quite down, and the lads were very disappointed with how we had played. We have high standards, and we don't like to see them drop. I think that was why we were a bit down straight after the game. We all hate losing", he said. Dominic Matteo later echoed Smith's comments in his book *In My Defence*. "We knew we'd had a lucky escape which was why the celebrations afterwards were more relief than joy on our part. It was certainly nothing like the nights in Milan and Rome, that's for sure. I almost felt sheepish going out to wave to the fans after we'd got changed. I felt like we'd picked someone's pocket".

Although his players felt they had somewhat underperformed despite progressing, O'Leary knew the scale of the achievement his inexperienced team had just produced. "I had worries over this game and while people criticised me for talking down the fact that we had a three-goal lead from the first-leg I knew what Deportivo were capable of. We're through to the semi-final, against all odds, and considering this is our first attempt at the Champions League, to have reached the last four of the greatest club competition in world football, is a truly marvellous achievement", the Leeds boss told Don Warters.

Elsewhere on the other side of Spain, a 1-0 win for Valencia meant it would be them and not Arsenal facing Leeds in the semi-finals. The other semi-finals would see a heavyweight bout between Real Madrid and Bayern Munich as they saw off Galatasaray and Manchester United respectively. The latter meant that Leeds United were now English football's last hope of European glory.

A Bridge Too Far

Vs Valencia

UEFA Champions League Semi-Final

European football for 2001-02 was secured after a 2-0 home win over Chelsea thanks to two quickfire goals late on from Robbie Keane and Mark Viduka. This was preceded by another 2-0 victory at Upton Park as Rio Ferdinand made a goalscoring return to West Ham United. It was the defender's third goal in five games. Ferdinand had admitted after his maiden goal against Deportivo that his getting on the scoresheet was overdue and that he should be chipping in with more goals when he went up for corners and free-kicks.

The pair of victories ensured Leeds could finish no lower than fifth and would at least be participating in the next season's edition of the UEFA Cup and any earlier fears of a summer break being cut short to compete in the unwanted Intertoto Cup were now unwarranted. I'm delighted we won't have to play in it and I wasn't keen on entering it anyway. The lads are very pleased to think they won't have to face me in June, and I'm glad that I'll have a bit of extra time with my family" O'Leary stated. Although another involvement in the Champions League was still the ultimate goal for the remaining three games of the Premier League season, European qualification was at least one less distraction as Elland Road prepared to host arguably its biggest game in its long and famous history. It was already known that should Leeds overcome Deportivo La Coruna either Arsenal or Valencia would lay in wait in the semi-finals as the draws for both rounds were completed together and Valencia's subsequent victory over The Gunners meant travelling Leeds fans were booking flights to Spain for the fourth time in the campaign rather than train tickets to London. Like Deportivo, Valencia was likened to The Whites for their exciting and fearless approach and were threatening to become a real force in the European game ahead of the quarter-finals. Valencia and Leeds United too could both draw some comparisons. Both clubs were formed in the same year (1919) and both enjoyed similar amounts of success up to 2001. Like Leeds they also had some European pedigree having lifted the Inter-Cities Fairs Cup twice in the 1960's and also the European Cup Winners Cup in 1980. Like Leeds, their greatest period of success domestically eventually resulted in relegation from the top tier in the 1980s before a resurgence in the nineties, and were now two of

the likely lads' looking to break the Status Quo of the hierarchy at home and in Europe – (Real Madrid and Barcelona for Valencia and Manchester United, Arsenal and Liverpool for Leeds). And now both teams were just a two-game shootout away from a European Cup Final. The two teams had met twice previously in United's maiden two European campaigns. Leeds had been involved in some feisty encounters in their very first European Inter-Cities Fairs Cup campaign in 1965-66. They had already prevailed in hot-tempered affairs against Torino and Lokomotiv Leipzig before hosting Valencia in the third round in a game the media would dub "The Battle of Elland Road". Both teams were ordered off the pitch for a cooling-off period of eleven minutes after 75 minutes of play with the score at 1-1. The contest had reached boiling point when Valencia goalkeeper Riverio Nito lashed out at United's Jack Charlton and a host of Valencia players surrounded Charlton before 'Big Jack' was kicked by Francisco Vidagany. Charlton ran behind the goal and chased Vidagany for 30 yards before retaliating with a boot of his own and a dozen police officers could do little to control the two fighting sets of players. Leeds manager Don Revie was displeased with the common theme of the club's first European games. "If this is European football, I nearly think we are better off out of it. Charlton would have to be a saint not to retaliate," he said after the game. Charlton was fined £50 for his actions but was at least available to play in the return leg a fortnight later. In a more amicable encounter, Leeds was heading for elimination on the away goals rule until local boy Mike O'Grady scored fifteen minutes from time to send Leeds through. As fate would have it, Leeds and Valencia were pipped together again in the third round of the following season's competition. Again, after a 1-1 Elland Road draw Leeds prevailed 2-0 in the Mestalla to progress to the quarter-finals with a 3-1 aggregate win but the two club's paths wouldn't cross again for another 34 years.

The other semi-final pitted two giants together in Bayern Munich and Real Madrid and looking back you could be forgiven for thinking Leeds had the most favourable opponents of the three. However, Valencia had been in this situation twelve months previously and triumphed over the mighty Barcelona to set up an all-Spanish final against Real Madrid. The showpiece in Paris however proved one step too far in a 3-0 defeat. In 2000-01, looking to go one step further, *Los Ches'* had topped both of their groups including drawing twice with Manchester United before eliminating Arsenal in the quarter-finals. So once again Leeds would need every ounce of the underdog spirit they had adopted so well in the competition if they were to progress to the San Siro final.

Valencia was managed by a wise old Argentinian coach in the form of Hector Cuper – a clean sheet specialist – who would move on to Inter Milan at the end of the season. Valencia had only conceded eight goals in Europe up to this stage with six shut-outs in 14 games. They like Leeds also had to overcome a qualifying round brushing aside Austrian outfit FC Tirol Innsbruck after finishing third in the league.

Valencia in contrast to Leeds was an experienced side with many elder statesmen in their ranks with several players at the footballer's typical peak age of late 20s and many more that had passed the 30-year milestone. It was common knowledge that a small ingredient of their recipe for success over the past couple of years was the players taking legal vitamin injections. These included iron, vitamins, and other minerals to help them through the packed fixture schedule that a European campaign brings to a team's season. The first leg was gameday number 50 for Valencia and 54 for Leeds.

Valencia boss Cuper was a lot more respectful in his pre-game assessment of Leeds than some of his counterparts had been throughout the campaign but still believed his team had what was needed to progress. "Leeds have eliminated a lot of good teams and if we lose to them, it will certainly be a reason to reflect on why. But I don't think the semi-final is the end of our Champions League trail. Experience is probably the big difference between the Valencia side of last season and this. We were the revelation, the surprise, last season nobody gave us a chance. The same can be said of Leeds this time so we have to cancel out our virtues and exploit their weaknesses. I think Arsenal have more individual talent but Leeds are superior in collective talent", Cuper stated.

The first leg fell on David O'Leary's 43rd birthday and he reflected that this game was probably the greatest occasion of his career to date and rallied that Leeds was not just in the last four to "make up the numbers". "We want to get into the final and if we get in it, we want to win it because we have the hunger to do it and we may never get the chance again", he said.

As if the chance of lifting European club football's holy grail wasn't enough – winning the Champions League presented perhaps an even more manageable chance of qualification for the next season's campaign despite their relentless pursuit of a third-place finish in the league. Leeds entered this tie of monumental proportions in white-hot form having won their last six Premier League games. However, the omens looked good for Valencia also, who had a perfect record of five out of five in European semi-finals. All 36,437 tickets for the home game sold out within hours and Peter Ridsdale claimed that ground could have been sold out three times over such was the interest. Elland Road's rickety old gantry on the West Stand was also housing the world's media as the game was screened on 54 television channels across the globe.

The eleven that started both legs in the quarter-finals again took the field for the semi-final and the first chance of the game came Leeds's way. A free-kick just outside the penalty area on the right-hand side parallel to the goal presented Ian Harte with an opportunity to repeat his heroics against Anderlecht and Deportivo. However, his left-footed strike was powerfully driven towards the top, far corner but was tipped over the crossbar by Spanish international goalkeeper Santiago Canizares. Leeds then came close from the resultant corner – also taken by Harte as it was driven across the face of goal but escaped a touch from first Ferdinand and then Viduka. Canizares was on hand again to deny Leeds, this time the notoriously goal-shy David Batty trying his luck from 25 yards. Batty only scored four goals in 211 appearances across his two spells at the club, none of which came in his second spell from 1998-2004. United's bright start had encouraged the home crowd, but Leeds then needed their own goalkeeper's heroics to keep the score goalless. Juan Sanchez played in a chipped cross towards the towering 6ft 5 frame of John Carew who executed a bicycle kick towards Nigel Martyn's bottom left-hand corner which the Leeds stopper got down well to save. Leeds was then saved by the crossbar later in the first half. After Martyn punched away a cross, an on-rushing Gaizka Mendieta headed back goalwards aiming to loop his header away from Harte who was protecting his goal line, but the ball stuck the crossbar and ricocheted away as all in white breathed a sigh of relief. Half-chances were presented to Harry Kewell, Lee Bowyer, and Alan Smith on separate occasions, but they each sliced their shots harmlessly away from the goal. Leeds again came close to breaking the deadlock shortly before the break. Another Harte free-kick was whipped in towards the far post where Kewell headed back across the face of the goal. Ferdinand first jumped ahead two Valencia markers but just as it seemed his header was moving away from goal it fell into the path of an unmarked Alan Smith who could only head wide from two yards out - although Ferdinand's touch perhaps made his task a lot more complicated. Martyn was needed to make a good save from Sanchez on the stroke of half-time and with that, a pulsating first-half ended goalless.

Chances were more at a premium in the second period and Leeds's best chance came and went when Canizares pulled off a magnificent one-handed save to prevent Dominic Matteo from repeating his San Siro heroics with a powerful goal-bound header from a Harte corner which had been helped along by Bowyer. Appeals from the Leeds players that the ball had crossed the line were correctly declined by world-renowned referee Pierluigi Collina. "I was certain my header was going in only for Canizares to pull off one of the greatest saves I have ever seen. The ball was heading for the bottom corner, and I'd set off celebrating thinking it was in" Matteo later said in his autobiography.

The home side kept pressing for the goal they so craved to pack in their luggage for the return trip to Spain the following week, but it wouldn't come. Smith snatched at a good opportunity half-volleying way over from close range and the crossbar denied Lee Bowyer's header after Canizares evacuated his goal to close down Smith - whose cross took an awkward bounce on the way to Bowyer. If Leeds couldn't take the home advantage and win the game, their next objective was not to concede an away goal which Valencia looked more likely to score in the closing stages. Carew scuffed a shot from a promising position wide of Martyn's goal before deep into added time, Ferdinand preserved a clean sheet for Leeds with a goal-line clearance as Vicente Rodriguez's shot into the ground looked to be nestling just under the crossbar. A goalless draw meant it was all to play for in the Mestalla a week later, but nobody could accuse Leeds of not going for the win having had 20 attempts on goal. In the other semi-final first-leg, Bayern Munich took a huge step towards the final defeating Real Madrid at the Bernabéu courtesy of a Gionni Eber goal.

"We would have liked to have scored a couple of goals, but we were up against a very good side. Valencia has good players and an excellent system. I don't think this tie is over. I am proud of my players because they gave their all. It's going to be tough for us in Spain. Valencia may not have been beaten at home for quite a while and they have a solid defence. But we're only 90 minutes away from a final appearance and that will drive us all on", O'Leary commented post-match.

***

In between the two legs was an assignment that was crucial to Leeds's third-place aspirations but was somewhat of an irritant to their European hopes as Leeds travelled to London to face Arsenal. Such a tricky game with no little jeopardy was the last thing O'Leary's side needed in between the club's biggest games in recent times. Leeds fans taunted the Highbury faithful letting them know of their upcoming midweek plans and making sure that Arsenal knew what they had missed out on with a chant of "What are you doing on Tuesday night?". The North Bank retorted with a quick-witted response - "You're going out on Tuesday Night". Goals from Freddie Ljungberg and Sylvain Wiltord put Arsenal 2-0 ahead before a reply from Ian Harte gave Leeds some hope. A harmful 2-1 defeat could not be avoided though much to O'Leary's frustration. "I always thought that the Arsenal game was the one that would cost us third place. We could have done without a game like this three days before a European semi-final," he said. But that wasn't to be the last of the circumstances affecting Leeds's chances in the second leg in Spain. Leeds had escaped any yellow cards in the home leg and therefore had no suspension worries. Or so they thought. The Leeds team had stayed at the Sopwell House Hotel in St.Alban's before they departed for Valencia instead of returning to Yorkshire. It was there, as O'Leary was preparing for the biggest game of his and his squad's careers that he received a call to inform him that any plans he was making would not be able to involve his most influential player from the campaign. Controversy once again surrounded Lee Bowyer as he was sanctioned with a three-match European ban after television replays spotted an incident in which Bowyer looked to have stamped on his opponent Victor Sanchez in the first leg. Despite the midfielder's off-pitch troubles his form over the season particularly in Europe was irrepressible and had a week earlier picked up the Supporter's Club player of the year and would add the club's official equivalent a week later.

UEFA's disciplinary committee had ruled that Leeds would be unable to appeal until three days after the game meaning Bowyer would not only be absent from the Mestalla clash - but if an appeal was unsuccessful – would miss the final too should Leeds get there. The frustrations over the decisions were only enhanced as on the pitch the most highly regarded referee in world football saw no infringement and the inconsistency from UEFA. In the other semi-final an arguably more obvious case of violent conduct went unpunished when Bayern Munich midfielder Mehmet Scholl had elbowed Real Madrid defender Michel Salgado in the face and Scholl escaped any further sanction.

It was a devastating blow for the Leeds and manager to deal with on the eve of the match. O'Leary later commented in *Leeds United on Trial*. "I was stunned. We couldn't afford to lose Lee, and it was a terrible blow for him as well as for our chances. We studied the video. It was ludicrous to claim that Lee had stamped on his opponent: the Valencia player had fallen underneath him, and the only genuine contact was when Bowyer initially trod on the Spaniard because he couldn't avoid him".

Dominic Matteo also later commented in his autobiography on the effect it had on the mindset of the Leeds team. "Bow's suspension came as a bitter blow to the team as well. Single players don't make a team but losing single players can knock a team sideways. I certainly feel that happened to us ahead of the semi-final second leg".

In a show of either eccentric team spirit, youthful frolicking, or as an attempt to intimidate the Valencia players, the Leeds team had shaved their heads with a number one buzz cut all over. The only exceptions of Ian Harte who didn't want to spoil his upcoming wedding photos and Bowyer and Jonathan Woodgate who opted out for fears of how they may be perceived in their legal proceedings.

Whatever the incentive behind the new haircuts it didn't impress the manager. "I didn't like it. I thought it was them being young and stupid. I went absolutely mad with them. They were young boys and they thought, 'Let's look lean and mean going into battle'. I'm not sure about that. I didn't approve. They thought I was an old prude", O'Leary said to *The Athletic* in 2021. The Spanish media painted a narrative of this Leeds team being nothing but a team of thugs and particularly picked out Matteo and Ferdinand who were, without substance, portrayed as the dirtiest players in the Premier League.

***

"It was just the longest day. From the moment we got up, kick-off seemed so far away. We went for a walk with the players, came back, had a meal together, and went back to our rooms. I remember sitting in my room for ages, looking at my notes, going over it in my mind". That was how O'Leary described his memory of Tuesday 8th May 2001 when speaking to *The Athletic* two decades later. His Leeds United side were just 90 minutes and a score draw or a win away from a place in the Champions League final in their first attempt. Leeds had reached the final once before in 1974-75 with their finest ever yet ageing team going agonisingly close to fulfilling a decade-long culmination of work with the holy grail. But fast forward to 2001 and this was different such had been the growth and worldwide interest in the competition and the riches it would bring. There was a big argument for this being the biggest game in the history of the football club. The Mestalla stadium was an imposing cathedral on Spain's East coast with its steep towering stands and fervent support from all angles of the arena. Valencia boss Hector Cuper had likened it to having "an English type of atmosphere" before the game and his managerial counterpart echoed that sentiment when O'Leary described

Valencia's home as having "an incredible atmosphere, where the crowd is packed in so tight it feels like it's on top of you". To make it more daunting, no English side had managed to win at the Mestalla since Leeds themselves in 1967. However, Leeds fans travelled in numbers in the hope and excitement of witnessing a famous night for their club. Approximately 6,000 fans travelled although demand exceeded supply and not all travelled with tickets.

The 'longest day' anxiety that O'Leary reflected upon on the build of the match had unfortunately seeped into his squad too. Dominic Matteo wrote in his autobiography, "I remember feeling something just wasn't right in the dressing room ahead of kick-off. The lads were unusually subdued and quiet. Usually, we were loud and bubbly. We were also very good at firing each other up ahead of a big game. But in Valencia, the atmosphere in what was a huge dressing room was almost eerie. Anyone wandering in would never have guessed we were about to play the biggest game of our lives", he wrote. Was it the enormity of what was at stake for this young side? The scale of the challenge? Or is the wind being taken out of their sails following the suspension of Bowyer so close to the game? Who knows, but it is now clear that the mentality, spirit, and morale that had gotten Leeds so far was missing when it was about to be needed most.

Both teams had five players walking a tightrope for suspension from the final. Leeds had Matteo, Batty, Smith, Dacourt, and Bakke whilst Valencia risked Roberto Ayala, Mauricio Pellegrino, David Albelda, captain Gaizka Mendieta, and midfielder Kily Gonzalez. Bowyer had travelled with the squad but was forced to watch from the dugout – looking pensive as he was helpless to assist his teammates complete a journey, he had been so instrumental in. Erik Bakke was the beneficiary of Bowyer's ban, being the one to come in and replace him in the only change from the first leg.

A great reception awaited the players with a display of the Champions League logo created from the vast, steep stands as the teams lined up for the pre-match anthem. Leeds started the game brightly enough defending astutely and breaking forward when they could. Their sensible game plan was clear knowing that one away goal would put them firmly in the driving seat. However, Martyn needed to make a save in the opening two minutes to deny Gaizka Mendieta, and the deadlock in the tie was broken as early as fifteen minutes in and in controversial fashion. Juan Sanchez converted Medieta's cross, diving to reach the ball but turning the ball goalwards with his left arm which went unnoticed by Swiss referee Urs Meier. Martyn and Ferdinand closest to the incident immediately protested Sanchez's violation but for the second time in the competition, Leeds were left ruing a goal from a handball going unpunished in Spain after suffering the same fate from Raul Gonzalez away at Real Madrid. Leeds's first chance on goal was a speculative shot from distance by Harry Kewell which flew well over, and Olivier Dacourt then created an opportunity for himself to slalom through the midfield until his shot was aimed straight at Santiago Canizares. David Batty and Alan Smith also forced the Valencia goalkeeper into comfortable saves as Leeds began to find a foothold in the match.

As the teams went into the break three-quarters of the way through the tie, Leeds knew that Sanchez's controversial goal advantage was just as tentative to Valencia's hopes. One goal for the away side without reply in the second period would send them into the Champions League final. "We were putting Valencia under pressure, and their coach Hector Cuper, and their fans were clearly getting more and more agitated. At half-time, everyone in the dressing rooms was delighted with how things were going. All the players were convinced that we were going to score", said Eddie Gray in his autobiography.

However, those lofty second-half hopes all but ended immediately. Just two minutes after the restart Sanchez had doubled Valencia's lead – this time legitimately with a well-taken left-footed strike finding the bottom corner from 25 yards out. Five minutes later Mendieta well and truly put the final nail in the coffin of United's dreams of a return to Milan for the final. The influential captain who had been magnificent across both legs of the semi-final found himself in acres of space in the midfield and drove towards the Leeds defence before unleashing a strike just outside the penalty area past an outstretched Martyn. It was a fine way for him to mark his 300th appearance for the club. A resigned look on the face of David O'Leary told the story that the Mestalla was a bridge too far for his team. The woodwork denied Sanchez a hat-trick as he poked an effort past the onrushing Martyn and struck a post as Leeds couldn't wait for their torrid evening to end. United's frustrations reached a climax in the closing minutes when Smith was sent off for a petulant two-footed lunge on Vicente Rodriguez. The Leeds players had dropped to their knees on the final whistle perhaps knowing the biggest opportunity of many of their careers had died a death on this warm Spanish battlefield. The incredible and defiant support of the travelling Leeds fans had tried to lift their troops though with chants of "we'll support you ever more" and "we're Leeds and we're proud of it" ringing out.

Dominic Matteo, years later summed up the atmosphere in the dressing room post-game. "There were bodies strewn all over the place and a few were in tears. The lads knew we had let ourselves down. Several had frozen and I maintain to this day that the game was lost before kick-off when we were unusually uptight. I just wish it could have been different. In fact, that is the one game in my career where I would love to go back and play it again. Playing in a Champions League final would have been immense. It is a huge regret we did not perform anything like we could have". Dacourt was one of those in tears inconsolable at the missed opportunity. "I knew we were so close to winning the European Cup. At the end of the game, I had tears. You didn't think it was going to be over", Dacourt later told *The Athletic*. Erik Bakke who started the game only down to Bowyer's suspension still rued UEFA's decision as a deciding factor. "You had me, Oliver Dacourt, and David Batty in there, with me on the right. I wanted to play but I wasn't good on the right. We missed something on the night and if Lee had played, there would have been a bigger chance, I can't deny that", the Norwegian said.

The one player visibly upset the most in the Mestalla dressing room though was the twenty-year-old local boy Alan Smith, but he was given no sympathy from his irate manager after his late sending off. O'Leary could see the red mist coming in the closing stages of the match with Leeds chasing shadows at 3-0 down and wanted to substitute him but had no ideal attacking replacement. "It was down to young, competitive stupidity. I had a right go at him in the dressing room at the end. I walked in and saw Alan crying. I made him cry even more when I pointed out that he would feel really hurt the next season when the European games came around again, and he found himself suspended. What he did was no good for Alan Smith, for his team, or for me, his manager. I left him in no doubt about that", O'Leary stated less than a year on from the game in *Leeds United on Trial*. Time had mellowed his view on his reaction though when speaking to *The Athletic* in 2021. "I probably made a poor man-management decision there. We were losing and we could see he was getting frustrated. I should have taken him off at that point. Sometimes aggression got the better of Alan. But he was a winner."

Matters were made worse for the crestfallen Leeds squad when the police escort that would take their bus from the crowds of the stadium back to their hotel did not arrive and they were forced to sit through the joyous celebrations of the Valencia locals celebrating long into the night with car horns, fireworks and flares illuminating the night. All it needed was Jim Bowen from the 1980s gameshow Bullseye to stand at the front of the bus and say, "Let's have a look at what you could have won".

Leeds had now lost on all four trips to Spain, whereas they were unbeaten in every other country they travelled to. O'Leary was in a positive reflective mood to the media post-match summarising that "People are disappointed we are not in the Champions League final. That shows just how far we have come". In his next programme notes days later he added "Let's not forget that for the whole of the first leg and the first half of the match in Spain, we matched a team that has some superb individual players, and who are in the top two Champions League teams for the second year in a row. I thought we played really well up to half-time. I was very confident we could still go on and win the game even though we were behind to what I thought was a scandalous goal – Sanchez clearly deflected the ball into the net with his arm. Everything we have learned will make us stronger and stand us in good stead for next season. We've all had a wonderful time and can look back on some great memories. Long may it continue", stated the Leeds boss.

The European adventure lasted one day short of nine months and took in 17,100 miles. From the tough qualifying round against 1860 Munich in which a threadbare Leeds side got themselves over the line in the Olympiastadion, to the 'torrid initiation' at the Camp Nou. The incredible late win in the rain against AC Milan, the rout of Besiktas at home before standing strong on the unwanted return to Istanbul. Being seconds away from defeating the mighty Barcelona and Dom Matteo scoring a very good goal at the San Siro. Welcoming the Galactico's to Elland Road, Smith's winner in Rome, storming Anderlecht's impenetrable fortress and leading (for a couple of minutes at least) at the Bernabéu. Blowing away Deportivo before escaping an onslaught in Spain, all the way to Elland Road thinking Leeds had one foot in the final but for Canizares's stupendous save from Matteo. It had been one hell of a journey.

***

Although it would have come as little consolation at the time, on the same evening as the Valencia defeat, Leeds was dealt a favour by their former employee Jimmy Floyd Hasselbaink. His brace at Anfield earned Chelsea a 2-2 draw meaning Liverpool had dropped two crucial points in the race for third place and that was what Leeds's attention needed to quickly turn to if they wanted another ride on the Champions League rollercoaster with just two league games remaining – both at home. Already relegated Bradford City was next in line four days later and faced a Leeds side that unloaded all of their frustrations on their nearest neighbours with a 6-1 rout at Elland Road with six different players writing their names on the scoresheet. Going into the final day Leeds had to face a similar permutation to the previous season. Leeds hosted Leicester City knowing they would need to win and hope that Liverpool would fail to win at The Valley against Charlton Athletic. At half-time, both Leeds and Liverpool were being held (1-1 and 0-0 respectively) but whilst a brace from Smith and a goal from Harte gave Leeds a 3-1 win in the second half, Liverpool ran riot and secured third place with a 4-0 win. Despite winning eight out of their final nine league games, Leeds finished in fourth place one point shy of the Champions League places and would have to settle for a place in the UEFA Cup in 2001-02. Looking at the league table Leeds were only twelve points of Champions Manchester United despite their mid-season worries of getting caught up in a relegation scrap. It was though still one of the most memorable and successful campaigns in the recent history of Leeds United Football Club. At this point, it seemed like just the beginning for this exciting young team. Eddie Gray was part of the Don Revie dynasty in the 1960s and 70s and could see history repeating itself. "The defeat in Spain was not the end; it was the beginning. I can honestly see no reason why the club should not establish the same record that was achieved in the Revie years", Gray said in his 2001 autobiography. Little did anyone know; Elland Road was like the Titanic heading for the iceberg. It was the beginning of the end.

Epilogue

We Lived the Dream

"Should we have spent so heavily in the past? Probably not. But we lived the dream. We enjoyed the dream. Only by making the right decisions today, can we rekindle the dream in the future".

Fast forward twenty months from Leeds United's appearance in the Champions League semi-final and these were the words from Peter Ridsdale defending the decision to sell Jonathan Woodgate to Newcastle United in January 2003. To his left was his manager Terry Venables, staring ahead with a grimace almost too disgusted to sit and listen to his boss address the press. The warning signs were not immediately clear, but Leeds were now no longer a team on the up but a team fighting for their Premier League survival and a club fighting for their survival full stop. A further failure in 2001-02 to secure Champions League qualification coupled with the continued frivolous spending in chasing the sun had caught up with the football club to the point of financial ruin. Their once enigmatic young team who was tipped to be a threat to Manchester United's dominance of English football but now resembled a carcass that vultures surrounded in droves cherry picking their pools of talent at cut prices.

Before things got worse, however, things continued to look up for Leeds and David O'Leary as the 2001-02 season started. United had picked themselves up from their double disappointment of Valencia and subsequently missing out on another go at the Champions League and started the season like a house on fire. Leeds went twelve games unbeaten at the start of the Premier League season taking them to the summit before succumbing 2-0 to Sunderland at the

Stadium of Light in mid-November. Leeds had managed to keep hold of all their star assets in the summer and collected no further signings but did extend their eye-watering spending in the opening half of the season signing Seth Johnson from Derby County for £7 million and a statement marquee signing in Robbie Fowler making the switch from Anfield to Elland Road for £12 million in November.

The court case involving several Leeds United players, particularly Lee Bowyer and Jonathan Woodgate that loomed over the football club for nearly two years finally concluded too. Beginning on October 8th 2001, and running through to December 14th the verdict concluded that Bowyer was found not guilty of all charges of grievous bodily harm (GBH) and affray whilst Woodgate was found not guilty of GBH but guilty of affray. Woodgate escaped a prison sentence but was ordered to complete 100 hours of community service. Of Woodgate's two Middlesbrough-based friends involved in the case, Neale Caveney received the same sentence of community service for affray, but Paul Clifford was sentenced to six years imprisonment for being found guilty of GBH and affray. Bowyer and Woodgate were imposed with a fine of four week's wages for a breach of club discipline. Bowyer who stressed his exoneration and innocence refused to pay and was duly placed on the transfer market. He was left out of a 3-2 win over Everton before being restored to the squad and scoring in a 3-4 defeat to Newcastle in a first versus second clash and restored his hero status with the fans netting a last-minute winner away at Southampton a week later. Despite being cleared of all charges; Bowyer later ended the long-running legal battle with the Najeib family by agreeing to an out-of-court settlement in 2005 with The Guardian reporting a package of £170,000.

On the pitch, no Premier League team had collected more points in the calendar year of 2001 than Leeds United, and on New Year's Day 2002 they sat proudly on top of the table following a 3-0 win over West Ham United. Things had never looked brighter for David O'Leary and his team. And then came Cardiff. A visit to third-tier Cardiff City and Ninian Park, whilst a potential banana skin, should have proved an insignificant obstacle for Leeds's FA Cup aspirations. However, a hot-tempered affair and a 2-1 defeat is widely reflected upon as the beginning of the end for this Leeds United team, at least on the footballing side. Despite taking an early lead through Mark Viduka, a red card for Alan Smith and a late Scott Young goal sent Leeds out in a game marred by crowd violence, in no small part induced by Cardiff owner Sam Hamman walking past and goading the Leeds United supporters. Hamman, the maverick Lebanese former chairman of Wimbledon's infamous crazy gang era, completed his role of the wind-up merchant by reeling in O'Leary after the match. After the draw for the Third Round was made, O'Leary opened himself up for potential ridicule stating that Leeds could start and finish their FA Cup campaign in Cardiff (where the finals were held during the rebuilding of Wembley stadium from 2001-2006). On exiting Ninian Park, Ridsdale reveals in his autobiography that he had to restrain O'Leary after Hamman taunted the Leeds boss shouting, "You're right about one thing, your FA Cup started and ended in Cardiff!". The unlikely defeat was the catalyst for a ten-game winless run which had demoted Leeds from first to sixth in the Premier League and elimination from the UEFA Cup following defeat to PSV Eindhoven in the Fourth Round. Their form picked up enough to secure a fifth consecutive European campaign but crucially their fifth-place finish meant again it would be the UEFA Cup and not the Champions League. In June 2002 David O'Leary was sacked after nearly four years as head coach of Leeds United. For Ridsdale the release and promotion of a book written by O'Leary titled *Leeds United on Trial* was a major mitigating factor in his dismissal. O'Leary also wrote a column in a tabloid newspaper in which his players were not spared from public criticism. *Leeds United on Trial* was published in January 2002. The News of the World serialized the story to an even wider audience. The title of the book was provocative and controversial. Peter Ridsdale had always insisted that some of Leeds United's players were on trial and not the football club itself. The book was all revealing from a manager who was criticising some players he was still managing and revealing secrets from what should have been sacred to the dressing room. For Ridsdale, the book which coincided with the dramatic drop in form at the turn of the year was the tipping point in his dismissal. It was claimed that he had lost the respect of the dressing room. In Ridsdale's autobiography, he stated, "TEN players, either directly or indirectly through their agents, said they would be looking to move elsewhere if O'Leary remained as manager for the 2002-03 season". O'Leary years later admitted in hindsight he shouldn't have written the book. Yet again, Martin O'Neil, now at Glasgow Celtic, was at the top of Leeds's wish list for their new manager but contractual obligations at Parkhead prevented him from taking up the position. Instead replacing O'Leary was the popular Terry Venables, who six years previously almost led England to Euro 96 glory. However, one of 'El Tel's' first tasks was managing the departure of his star defender. Rio Ferdinand again broke the British transfer record less than two years after his move from West Ham to Leeds. This time however he would be moving from Leeds to arch-rivals Manchester United for an eye-watering £30 million. The warning signs would have been there for Venables however when the vast sum incoming for a star asset was not available for incomings. Only Nick Barmby (£2.75 million from Liverpool, Paul Okon (a free transfer from Middlesbrough), and Teddy

Lukic (a loan from Swedish side AIK Solna) came through the door - a stark contrast in ambition than shown in recent seasons. Leeds was still tipped to challenge for honours in 2002-03 though and started the season well with two 3-0 victories over newly promoted couple Manchester City (home) and West Bromwich Albion (away). They briefly topped the table after finally defeating a Manchester United side involving Ferdinand at Elland Road in September, but by Christmas, they were potential relegation contenders. It was now clear that Leeds United was in financial trouble and resembling a sinking ship. Robbie Keane was sold to Tottenham Hotspur in late August for £7 million - the first loss made on a transfer from O'Leary and Ridsdale's spending spree whilst chasing the dream. A few months into the season a key member of the Champions League run - Olivier Dacourt - was loaned to Roma at the insistence of Venables after he was unimpressed with the attitude and application of the Frenchman and felt he was undermining his authority. "If he wants to go to Italy - and if someone is interested - I will personally drive him there", Venables said at the time. January 2003 saw the opening of the inaugural transfer window where players could only be bought and sold within designated periods in the summer close season and in this case the month of January. Leeds's talented squad was torn apart at minimal prices much like a bankrupt aristocrat's belongings being auctioned off. Leeds was in no position to bargain, and the footballing world knew it, yet some of the deals were exasperating for Leeds United supporters to comprehend. Fowler was sold to Manchester City for half the price they paid for him in a deal which inexplicably meant Leeds were still paying a portion of his wages. Lee Bowyer, after the ordeal the months earlier following the conclusion of his court case was offered a five-year contract from Leeds which he subsequently turned down. A deal was agreed in the summer of 2002 for a £9 million switch to Liverpool which broke down due to a disagreement on Bowyer's wage demands. Months later, he was sold for next to nothing in a £100,000 to West Ham. The straw that broke the camel's back as far as Leeds fans were concerned was the sale of Jonathan Woodgate to Newcastle United for £9 million. Leeds supporters knew that outgoings were necessary for their situation but were promised by the board that Leeds would "not be selling the family silver". Woodgate was now considered the jewel in the crown and so when he too was sold the fans sensed the situation was even more serious than initially appeared with reports that debts were in the region of £80 million and wanted answers. It wasn't just supporters asking the questions but their manager too. "There was no sensitivity to the football side. Take a look, the soul is being ripped out here," Venables said in a later interview. It was this particular sale that led to Ridsdale's infamous 'we lived the dream' press conference.

With Leeds sliding towards relegation into the Football League, decisions were made. On March 21st Venables and Leeds United parted company by mutual consent with Leeds following an FA Cup quarter-final defeat to lower league Sheffield United and five defeats in six league games leaving United languishing in 15th place and seven points above the drop zone. A week later Ridsdale's untenable tenure as chairman was over when he handed in his resignation with non-executive director Professor John McKenzie taking over as chairman. Under Ridsdale's custodianship Leeds had taken out a loan of £60 million against future season ticket sales and one of McKenzie's first acts as chairman was to reveal the details of some of the lavish expenditures Leeds United was indulging in non-footballing interests. A £280 per year bill for tropical goldfish in the chairman's office became a laughable symbol of the club's profligacy and a metaphorical stick for rival fans to beat Leeds with.

Former Sunderland manager Peter Reid was given the unenviable task of preserving Leeds's top-flight status with eight games to go on a caretaker basis. Reid secured thirteen points out of a possible 24 and survival was confirmed after a heroic 3-2 victory away to title-challenging Arsenal. Reid was awarded the position permanently ahead of the 2003-04 season but Leeds United was far from out of the woods. Harry Kewell was the next to leave in yet another disgraceful move from a business point of view. Kewell left for Liverpool at the low price of £5 million for a player of his talents and age and it was alleged at the time that £2 million of which would go directly to his agent Bernie Mandie – which Kewell later took legal action on. All Reid was able to bring in were a host of unproven loan moves from across the UK and the continent. The highest profile of which – Champions League and World Cup winning defender Roque Junior proving perhaps the least productive. Reid was sacked with Leeds in bottom place on 8th November 2003 following a 6-1 defeat away at Portsmouth – the club's worst league defeat since 1959. Club legend and assistant manager throughout the Champions League run Eddie Gray stepped in as caretaker manager for the remainder of the season but could not prevent what seemed like an inevitable relegation as control of the club changed hands twice more from Professor John McKenzie to Trevor Birch and then Gerald Krasner.

The rapid fall from grace is perhaps football's most famous comparison to the Greek myth of Icarus who flew too close to the sun and whose wings got burnt. Relegation from the Premier League would only be the beginning of the club's problems as they faced a 16-year exile from the Premier League that included numerous disastrous ownerships, two administrations, a total of 25 points deducted for administrative sanctioning, enduring three years in the third tier (the first time in the club's history), Elland Road and their Thorp Arch training ground was sold to raise funds and a further fourteen permanent managers took the hot seat before Marcelo Bielsa restored their top-flight status in 2020. All of which would need a series of books on itself to detail. In suffering relegation when they did Leeds had missed the gravy train. Premier League broadcast money jumped from a share of £1.1 billion to £5.136 billion in the period Leeds was ostracised from the top flight and a hierarchy of clubs such as the current big-six had almost monopolised the league's top positions Leeds had once occupied regularly. Leeds have never returned close to the heights of the early 2000s but is at least a financially stable football club once more.

However, despite the somber ending to this story, this book aims to portray itself as a celebratory account of a unique and thrilling period in the history of Leeds United Football Club and to remember one of the 'hipper' stories of the UEFA Champions League. FourFourTwo magazine rated Leeds United in 2000-01 2nd in their ranking of the 20 best cult Champions League sides ever in 2023 explaining that the team "remains one of the most exciting English sides of the modern era". There is no doubt that the financial irresponsibility whilst playing out this period was an overwhelming contributory factor to one of the biggest falls from grace of modern-day football. 'Doing a Leeds' is now a well-known term in English football, a phrase which is synonymous with the potentially dire consequences for domestic clubs in financial mismanagement which also has its own Wikipedia page. Each Leeds United supporter would have their viewpoint of how they look back on the period of the early 2000s and also those of the players involved. You would also probably have to ask supporters of Birmingham City, Swansea City, and Wigan Athletic. Their League Cup and FA Cup wins respectively at the beginning of the 2010s are more than Leeds United have managed in over three decades now. But would they trade the memories of those Wembley glories for the journey that Leeds enjoyed in

2000-2001 where they could almost reach out and touch the famous European Cup? Oliver Dacourt despite enjoying glory elsewhere later in his career with Inter Milan compared what Leeds had achieved to being better than tangible silverware when speaking to *The Athletic* in 2019. "We didn't win anything. That's true and it's a pity. I wish that we had. But as a team, we stay in the memory, don't we? And maybe the memories are more important than trophies", Dacourt said, "Maybe they're the best. You can laugh at me, but you have teams who won trophies, but nobody remembers them. Only the proper fans remember anything about them. If you say Leeds, everyone knows the Champions League. Everyone knows it. They know Leeds, they know 2001, they know what happened. In France, in Italy, people remember that team. I can tell you this for sure because I still have those conversations. I won nothing at Leeds, and at Inter, we won lots of trophies. But my time at Leeds was the best of my life. Because everyone felt alive."

Dacourt's reflections are echoed by many of his teammates too. Ian Harte, Dominic Matteo, and Danny Mills reflected upon "loving the journey" to UEFA.tv in 2021. "I wouldn't change that season for anything I don't think. Playing against the best in Europe in one season. I think some of the best times we ever had at the club", Mills stated. Harte echoed the sentiment speaking to *FourFourTwo* magazine in 2024. "Leeds supporters still love reminiscing about that season to this day, and I get goosebumps when I think about beating Deportivo. It was an amazing achievement to go so far", he said.

Peter Ridsdale took the mantra of the fall guy and will perhaps always be remembered as the villain to Leeds United supporters and his "we lived the dream" comments were ridiculed at the time and became a motto of the fall from grace story Leeds's promising period became. But after nearly a quarter of a century are those words now more aligned? Is it better to have lived the dream, and suffered, than to never have lived the dream at all?

Statistics

Leeds United UEFA Champions League 2000/01

Player	Position	Appearances (used as sub)	Goals
Nigel Martyn	Goalkeeper	12	0
Paul Robinson	Goalkeeper	6	0
Gary Kelly	Defender	11 (1)	0
Dominic Matteo	Defender	15	2
Michael Duberry	Defender	4	0
Lucas Radebe	Defender	10	0
Ian Harte	Defender	17	4
Jonathan Woodgate	Defender	5	0
Rio Ferdinand	Defender	7	1
Danny Hay	Defender	0 (1)	0
Gareth Evans	Defender	0 (1)	0
Danny Mills	Defender	15 (1)	0
Erik Bakke	Midfielder	10 (2)	1
Olivier Dacourt	Midfielder	14	0
Lee Bowyer	Midfielder	15	6
Alan Maybury	Midfielder	1	0
Matthew Jones	Midfielder	1	0
Jacob Burns	Midfielder	3(1)	0
David Batty	Midfielder	7 (1)	0
Jason Wilcox	Midfielder	2 (3)	1
Stephen McPhail	Midfielder	1 (2)	0
Harry Kewell	Midfielder	6 (3)	0
Mark Viduka	Striker	16	4
Michael Bridges	Striker	4	0

Alan Smith	Striker	16	7
Darren Huckerby	Striker	0 (2)	1
Tony Hackworth	Striker	0 (2)	0

Wednesday, August 9th, 2000 – Elland Road, Leeds

Leeds United 2-1 TSV 1860 Munich

Leeds United: Martyn, Kelly, Duberry, Radebe, Harte, Bakke, Dacourt, Bowyer, Smith, Viduka, Bridges (Mills 80). Subs not used: Huckerby, McMaster, Molenaar, G Evans, Hackworth, Robinson

Goals: Smith 39, Harte 71 (Pen)

TSV 1860 Munich: Hoffmann, Cerny, Zelic, Kurz, Stranzl (Winkler 82), Hassler, Votava, Mykland, Bierofka (Passlack 46), Agostino, Max. Subs not used: Borimirov, Reidi, Ehlers, Jentsch, Beierie

Goal: Agostino 90+3

Att: 33,769 **Referee:** Costas Kapitanis (Cyprus)

Bookings: Bakke, Dacourt, Smith (Leeds). Kurz, Votava (1860 Munich)

Sent off: Dacourt, Bakke (Leeds). Zelic (1860 Munich)

Wednesday, August 23rd, 2000 – Olympic Stadium, Munich

TSV 1860 Munich 0-1 Leeds United 1 (Leeds United win 2-1 on aggregate)

TSV 1860 Munich: Hoffmann, Passlack (Wintler 63), Kurz, Borimirov (Beierie 78), Max, Hassler, Cerny, Mykland, Stranzl, Agostino, Bierofka (Tyce 74). Subs not used: Jentsch, Greilich, Reidi, Ehlers.

Leeds United: Martyn, Kelly, Woodgate, Duberry, Harte, Bowyer, Jones (Evans 74), Radebe, Mills, Smith, Viduka. Subs not used: Bridges, Huckerby, Molenaar, McMaster, Hackworth, Robinson.

Goal: Smith 46

Att: 56,000 **Referee:** Claus Larsen (Denmark)

Bookings: None

Wednesday, September 13th, 2000 – Camp Nou, Barcelona

FC Barcelona 4-0 Leeds United

FC Barcelona: Dutruel, Abelardo, De Boer, Cocu (Petit 54), Simoa, Rivaldo (Alfonso 73), Gerard, Sergi, Overmars, Kluivert, Dani (De La Pena 65). Subs not used: Reizeger, Santamaria, Fernando, Arnau.

Goals: Rivaldo 9, De Boer 20, Kluivert 75, 83

Leeds United: Martyn, Kelly, Duberry, Radebe (Hay 89), Mills, Bowyer, Dacourt, McPhail (Hackworth 73), Harte, Bridges, Smith. Subs not used: Huckerby, Jones, Evans, Burns, Robinson

Att: 85,000 **Referee:** Markus Merk (Germany)

Bookings: Kluivert (Barcelona). Mills, Smith (Leeds)

Tuesday, September 19th, 2000, Elland Road, Leeds

Leeds United 1-0 AC Milan

Leeds United: Martyn, Kelly, Mills, Duberry, Harte, Bowyer, Bakke, Dacourt, Matteo, Smith, Bridges. Subs not used: Huckerby, Jones, Hay, Burns, Evans, Hackworth, Robinson.

Goal: Bowyer 89

AC Milan: Dida, Chamont, Costacurta, Maldini, Helveg, Albertini, Guinti, Coco, Shevchenko, Bierhoff, Guly (De Ascentis 59). Subs not used: Rossi, Leonardo, Roque Junior, Serginho, Sala, Saudali.

Att: 35,398 **Referee:** Gunter Benko (Austria)

Bookings: Bakke, Mills (Leeds), Coco, Maldini (Milan)

Tuesday, September 26th, 2000, Elland Road, Leeds

Leeds United 6-0 Besiktas

Leeds United: Martyn, Kelly, Mills, Radebe, Harte, Bowyer, Bakke, Dacourt (McPhail 76), Matteo, Smith (Huckerby 81), Viduka. Subs not used: Bridges, Burns, Hay, Jones, Robinson.

Goals: Bowyer 7, 90+, Viduka 12, Matteo 22, Bakke 65, Huckerby 90

Besiktas: Shorunmu, Erman (Rahim 83), Umtit, Khlestov, Nihat, Karhan, Tayfur, Ibrahim (Mehmet 74), Munch, Nouma (Fazli 72), Ahmet, Dursun. Subs not used: Fevzi, Murat, Bayram, Yasin.

Att: 34,485 **Referee:** Victor Pereira (Portugal)

Bookings: Bakke, Dacourt, Smith (Leeds). Erman Guracar, Tayfur Havutcu, Uzulmez (Besiktas)

Wednesday, October 18th, 2000, Inonu Stadium, Istanbul

Besiktas 0-0 Leeds United

Besiktas: Shorunmu, Ali Eren (Murat 63), Umtit, Khlevstov. Karhan, Mehmet (Ayhan 80), Tayfur, Munch, Yasin, Nihat, Ahmet, Dursun (Ibrahim 80). Subs not used: Rahim, Bayram, Ilhan, Fevzi.

Leeds United: Robinson, Kelly, Woodgate, Mills, Harte, Bowyer, Bakke, Burns, Matteo, Viduka, Bridges (Hukerby 27, McPhail 85). Subs not used: Jones, Hay, Evans, Hackworth, Milosevic.

Att: 20,000 **Referee:** J Wegereef (Holland)

Bookings: None

Tuesday, October 24th, 2000, Elland Road, Leeds

Leeds United 1-1 FC Barcelona

Leeds United: Robinson, Kelly, Woodgate, Mills, Harte, Bowyer, Dacourt (Burns 75), Bakke, Matteo, Smith, Viduka. Subs not used: McPhail, Jones, Hackworth, Evans, Hay, Milosevic.

Goal: Bowyer 4

FC Barcelona: Dutruel, Puyol, Reizeger (Dani 66), Abelardo, Simao, Xavi, Cocu, Sergi, Alfonso, Rivaldo, Luis Enrique (Gerard 66). Subs not used: De Boer, De La Pena, Gabri, Santamaria, Arnau

Goal: Rivaldo 90+

Att: 36,729 **Referee:** Terje Hauge (Norway)

Bookings: None

Wednesday November 9th, 2000, San Siro, Milan

AC Milan 1-1 Leeds United

AC Milan: Dida, Roque Junior, Chamot, Maldini, Helveg, Albertini, Gattuso, Serginho, Leonardo (Boban 54), Bierhoff, Shevchenko. Subs not used: Jose Mari, Ambrosini, Guly, Sala, Cocu, Abbiati.

Goal: Serginho 68

Leeds United: Robinson, Kelly, Radebe, Mills, Harte, Bowyer, Bakke, Dacourt, Matteo, Smith, Viduka. Subs not used: Jones, Hay, Maybury, Evans, Milosevic.

Goal: Matteo 44

Att: 52,289 **Referee:** Kim Nielsen (Denmark)

Bookings: Dacourt (Leeds)

Final Group H Standings

TEAM	P	W	D	L	GF	GA	PTS	GD	Qualification
AC Milan	6	3	2	1	12	8	11	+6	Advance to the second group stage
Leeds Utd	6	2	3	1	9	6	9	+3	Advance to the second group stage
FC Barcelona	6	2	2	2	13	9	8	+4	Transfer to UEFA Cup
Besiktas	6	1	1	4	4	17	4	-13	Eliminated from European Competition

Wednesday November 22nd, 2000, Elland Road, Leeds

Leeds United 0-2 Real Madrid

Leeds United: Robinson, Mills, Radebe, Woodgate, Harte, Kelly, Bowyer, Burns (Wilcox 60), Matteo, Viduka, Smith. Subs not used: Huckerby, Jones, Maybury, Molenaar, Evans, Milosevic.

Real Madrid: Casilla, Geremi, Hierro, Helguera, Roberto Carlos, Figo (Savio 89), Makelele, McMananaman, Guti (Munitis 88), Raul, Ivan Campo. Subs not used: Salgado, Morientes, Flavio.

Goals: Hierro 66, Raul 68.

Att: 36,794 **Referee:** Dick Jol (Holland)

Bookings: Bowyer, Smith, Woodgate (Leeds). Figo, Guti, Hierro (Real Madrid)

Tuesday, December 5th, 2000, Olympic Stadium, Rome

Lazio 0-1 Leeds United

Lazio: Peruzzi, Pancaro, Nesta, Couto, Favalli, Lombardo (Gottardi 82), Veron (Ravenelli 70), Simeone, Nedved, Crespo, Salas. Subs not used: Marchegiani, Mihajlovic, Colonesse, Negro, Pasaresi.

Leeds United: Robinson, Kelly, Radebe, Woodgate, Matteo, Bowyer, Dacourt, Bakke, Wilcox (Kewell 75), Smith, Viduka. Subs not used: Milosevic, Mills, Harte, Burns, Huckerby, Maybury.

Goal: Smith 80

Att: 42,450 **Referee:** Claude Colombo (France)

Bookings: Veron (Lazio). Bowyer, Viduka (Leeds)

Tuesday, February 13th, 2001, Elland Road, Leeds

Leeds United 2-1 Anderlecht

Leeds United: Martyn, Harte, Radebe, Ferdinand, Mills, Bowyer, Batty, Dacourt (Bakke 72), Matteo (Kewell 53), Smith, Viduka. Subs not used: Woodgate, Wilcox, Burns, Robinson.

Goals: Harte 77, Bowyer 86

Anderlecht: Milojevic, Crasson, Dheedene, Ilic, De Boeck, Vanderhaeghe, Stoica, Baseggio, Goor, Koller, Radzinski. Subs not used: Van Dieman, Hasi, Pirard, Dindane, Youls, Traore, Carlier.

Goal: Stoica 64

Att: 36, 064 **Referee:** Karl-Erik Nilsson (Sweden)

Bookings: Bowyer (Leeds). De Boeck (Anderlecht)

Wednesday, February 21st, 2001, Vanden Stock Stadium, Brussels

Anderlecht 1-4 Leeds United

Anderlecht: Milojevic, Crasson, De Boeck, Ilic (Dindane 40), Dheedene, Vanderhaeghe, Baseggio, Goor, Stoica, Koller, Radzinski. Subs not used: Carlier, Traore, Van Dieman, Youla, Pirard, Hasi.

Goal: Koller 76

Leeds United: Martyn, Mills, Ferdinand, Radebe, Harte, Batty, Bakke, Dacourt, Matteo, Smith, Viduka (Kewell 83). Subs not used: Hay, Wilcox, Maybury, Robinson.

Goals: Smith 13,38, Viduka 34, Harte (pen) 81

Att: 28,000 **Referee:** Rune Pedersen (Norway)

Bookings: Basseggio (Anderlecht), Harte, Mills (Leeds)

Tuesday, March 6th, 2001, Santiago Bernabéu Stadium, Madrid

Real Madrid 3-2 Leeds United

Real Madrid: Cesar, Geremi, Hierro, Karanka, Solari, Makelele (Savio Bortolini 87), Celades, McManaman, Figo, Morientes (Munitis 75), Raul. Subs not used: Casillas, Salgado, Guti, Tote.

Goals: Raul 7, 59, Figo 41

Leeds United: Martyn, Harte, Radebe (Kelly 65), Ferdinand, Matteo, Bakke (Wilcox 85), Dacourt, Batty, Kewell, Smith, Viduka. Subs not used: Robinson, Burns, Maybury.

Goals: Smith 6, Viduka 54

Att: 40,000 **Referee:** Ryszard Wojcik (Poland)

Bookings: Figo, Makelele (Real Madrid), Batty, Kewell (Leeds).

Wednesday 14th March 2001, Elland Road, Leeds

Leeds United 3-3 Lazio

Leeds United: Robinson, Kelly, Harte, Mills, Matteo, Bowyer, Burns, Maybury, Wilcox, Viduka (Hackworth 64), Kewell. Subs not used: Dacourt, Woodgate, Hay, Milosevic

Goals: Bowyer 28, Wilcox 43, Viduka 62

Lazio: Marchegiani, Colonnese, Mihajlovic, Couto, Stankovic, Castroman (Ruggiu 88), Bronio, Pesaresi, Nedved, Claudio Lopez (Salas 74), Ravanelli. Subs not used: Orlandoni, Negro, Crespo, Pancaro, Luciani

Goals: Ravanelli 21, Mihajlovic 29 (pen), 90

Att: 36,741 **Referee:** Konrad Plautz (Austria)

Bookings: Matteo (Leeds), Castroman, Colonnese, Stankovic (Lazio)

Final Group D Standings

TEAM	P	W	D	L	GF	GA	PTS	GD	Qualification
Real Madrid	6	4	1	1	14	9	13	+5	Advance to the knockout stage
Leeds Utd	6	3	1	2	12	19	10	+2	Advance to the knockout stage

Anderlecht	6	2	0	4	7	12	6	-5	Eliminated
Lazio	6	1	2	3	9	11	5	-2	Eliminated

Wednesday, April 4th, 2001, Elland Road, Leeds

Leeds United 3-0 Deportivo La Coruna

Leeds United: Martyn, Mills, Ferdinand, Matteo, Harte, Bowyer, Dacourt, Batty, Kewell (Wilcox 84), Smith, Viduka. Subs not used: Robinson, Kelly, Bakke, Burns, Maybury

Goals: Harte 27, Smith 51, Ferdinand 66

Deportivo La Coruna: Molina, Manuel Pablo, Romero, Naybet, Cesar, Scaloni (Tristan 72), Emerson, Duscher (Valeron 55), Fran (Pandiani 71), Djalminha, Makaay. Subs not used: Songo'o, Devila, Victor, Fernando, Sanchez.

Att: 35, 508 **Referee:** Gilles Veissiere (France)

Bookings: Dacourt, Batty, Matteo (Leeds), Emerson (Deportivo).

Wednesday, April 17th, 2001, Riazor Stadium, Coruna

Deportivo La Coruna 2-0 Leeds United (Leeds United win 3-2 on aggregate)

Deportivo La Coruna: Molina, Manuel Pablo, Romero, Naybet, Mauro Silva, Djalminha (Valeron 69), Fran, Pandiani (Turu Flores 79), Victor (Tristan 62), Donato, Makaay. Subs not used: Robinson, Wilcox, Burns, Maybury.

Goals: Djalminha 9 (pen), Tristan 73

Leeds United: Martyn, Mills, Ferdinand, Matteo, Harte, Bowyer, Dacourt, Batty, Kewell (Bakke 77), Smith, Viduka. Subs not used: Robinson, Wilcox, Burns, Maybury.

Att: 35,600 **Referee:** Stefano Braschi (Italy)

Bookings: Ferdinand, Martyn (Leeds)

Wednesday, May 2nd, 2001, Elland Road, Leeds

Leeds United 0-0 Valencia

Leeds United: Martyn, Mills, Harte, Ferdinand, Matteo, Bowyer, Dacourt, Batty, Kewell, Viduka, Smith. Subs not used: Robinson, Kelly, Woodgate, McPhail, Wilcox, Bakke, Burns.

Valencia: Canizares, Angloma, Pellegrino, Ayala, Carboni, Albelda, Baraja, Mendieta, Kily Gonzalez (Vicente 89), Juan Sanchez (Zahovic 67) Carew. Subs not used: Palop, Deschamps, Djukic, Aimar, Aurelio.

Att: 36, 437 **Referee:** Pierluigi Collina (Italy)

Bookings: Baraja, Carboni (Valencia)

Wednesday, May 8th, 2001, Mestella Stadium, Valencia

Valencia 3-0 Leeds United (Valencia CF win 3-0 on aggregate)

Valencia: Canizares, Angloma, Ayala, Pellegrino, Aurelio, Albelda, Mendieta (Angulo 73), Aimar (Deschamps 70), Kily Gonzale (Vicente 65), Carew, Juan Sanchez. Subs not used: Palop, Djukic, Zahovic, Alonso.

Goals: Juan Sanchez 15, 46, Mendieta 52

Leeds United: Martyn, Mills, Ferdinand, Matteo, Harte, Bakke, Dacourt, Batty, Kewell, Viduka, Smith. Subs not used: Robinson, Kelly, Woodgate, McPhail, Wilcox, Burns, Maybury.

Att: 53,000 **Referee:** Urs Mejer (Switzerland)

Bookings: Aimar, Juan Sanchez (Valencia)

Sent off: Smith (Leeds)

Sources

Books

Coomber, Richard, *Lucas – From the Streets of Sowetto to Soccer Superstar*, (Great Northern Books, 2010).

Gray, Eddie, *Marching on Together – My Life at Leeds United*, (Hodder and Stoughton, 2001).

Jarred, M & Macdonald, M, *Leeds United, The Complete European Record,* (The Breedon Books Publishing Company Limited, 2003).

Matteo, Dominic, *In My Defence, The Autobiography*, (Great Northern Books, 2011).

O'Leary, David, *Leeds United On Trial – The Inside Story of an Astonishing Year,* (Little, Brown 2002).

Ridsdale, Peter, *United We Fall – Boardroom Truths About the Beautiful Game*, (MacMillan, 2007).

Sutcliffe, Richard, *Marching on Together – Leeds United in Europe 2000-2001* (Terrace Banter, Scotland, 2001).

Warters, Don, *2001 A European Odyssey – Leeds United's UEFA Champions League (*Leeds United Publishing LTD).

Websites

BBC.co.uk

BBC Sport

Footballdatabase.eu

FourFourTwo.com

fussballstadt.com

Leedsunited.com

Sportspromedia.com

The Athletic

The Guardian

The Independent

The Irish Times

UEFA.com

YouTube

Magazines

FourFourTwo

Leeds Leeds Leeds Magazine – January 2001, April 2001, June 2001

Leeds United in Europe – 2000

Leeds United FC Matchday Programmes 1998-99, 1999-00, 2000-01, 2010-11.

(All Leeds United Publishing Ltd)

Videos

ITV Sport (sourced from YouTube)

Leeds United – The Best of Europe – DVD – Leeds United FC

Leeds United Season Review – 1998/99, 1999/00

UEFA.tv

Authors Note

Born into a Leeds United supporting family, whose parents were married at Elland Road, writing this book has been a labour of love. I was seven years old when on the opening day of the 1999-00 season I took a sudden interest in the fortunes of my Dad's team and kneeled in front of the TV staring at *Teletext*, feeling the surge of anticipation as the page which was displaying the latest score of Leeds United V Derby County appeared and waiting to see the 0 change to a 1 on the side next to Leeds. It never did as the scoreline finished goalless. But I was hooked. Within weeks my jungle-themed bedroom I shared with my two younger brothers was plastered in Leeds posters snipped out of *MATCH Magazine* and I became indoctrinated in the rules and idiosyncrasies of football including arguing with a friend in the garden over which 'side' of the lawn was 'offside'. I identified most with Alan Smith. Not because of his homegrown prodigy status but because on a poster I had, he sported the same floppy haircut I had. When he switched to a more mature, shorter, spiky do, so did I. I was deterred from copying him and the team when they shaved their heads ahead of the Champions League semi-final in Valencia. In my first couple of years as a Leeds United supporter, I saw the most exciting young team in the country and perhaps Europe, finish in third place in the Premier League, make two European semi-finals, and had to learn the ins and outs of why my team was making the front page of the newspaper for the arrest of two of my heroes and then the digest the news of the murder of two of our supporters. By the time I had left school, Leeds United was in the depths of League One and lucky to have a team full stop due to financial difficulties.

In the depths of Leeds's sixteen-year exile from the Premier League, I had become frustrated and disillusioned if not apathetic to the fortunes of my team. Seeing other teams enjoying success irritated me and it was the memories of the Champions League run in 2000-01 that comforted me in those times. My thoughts were of how many teams would have killed for that journey and those memorable European nights. I felt it kept Leeds relevant at a time in which they were being left behind. The good times came back, although not to the same extent under Marcelo Bielsa from 2018-2022. It had been a long-term ambition of mine to write a book and when Bielsa was sacked in 2021 and it felt as though Leeds were back to square one it felt like the ideal time to take a deep dive back into my memories of the turn of the century. Writing the book has made me wish I could hop inside a time machine and relive the journey live at the games with an unlimited credit card. Or hope that the Leeds United of today could replicate a similar achievement. I don't know which of those is more realistic. Researching Leeds United's Champions League adventure has been a real revel in nostalgia. I hope it has been the same for you too.

Lawrence O'Sullivan

(April 2024)

Printed in Great Britain
by Amazon